JERICHO MARCH

A leadership journey with a God bigger

than you could ever expect

DOUGLAS MANN

FREILING

PUBLISHING

Published by Freiling Publishing, a division of Freiling Agency, LLC.

P.O. Box 1264,
Warrenton, VA 20188

www.FreilingPublishing.com

ISBN 978-1-950948-37-6

Printed in the United States of America

DEDICATION

This book is dedicated to my beautiful wife, Michelle, who has been my faithful partner and better half in this Jericho March called life. It has not always been easy, but our commitment to march together through thick and thin has remained steadfast. I love you.

It is written for my children, Andrew, Abby, and Elly, so that they may know a bit of my life's path and better understand that true leadership only comes through serving others.

Finally, I write with great thanks to Mike Jeffries and Steve Elliott - the two men who taught me that a lifetime of serving the Lord can be serious fun. To all the other friends I've made along the way, some mentioned in these pages and some not, you are the ones who have made this life extraordinary. Thank you.

Fabula est vestri…

Table of Contents

PROLOGUE

I imagine there is not a firstborn who grows up aspiring to be a servant.

From the day I was born until the present, I have felt the expectation of being a leader. That feeling has hung like a dark and troubling cloud over my life. Am I living up to expectations? The expectations of my parents, those of my wife and children, my boss, my pastor, or strangers I don't even know? Most of these expectations aren't real. They are constructs of many years of warped thinking patterns that have now carved out rugged, familiar grooves in my life, just like a wagon train traversing a well-known route across a desolate prairie.

It is odd how "wrong thinking" can trap a person into repeating cycles that he or she doesn't realize need to be broken. I am not referring to addictions or sinful behaviors that should be easily recognizable as ungodly. I'm suggesting character traits that people, Christians included, usually characterize as admirable.

"Wow, he sure is a gifted leader."

"That guy sure knows how to take charge and get things done!"

This was the trap to which I succumbed. Anyone can serve, right? It takes real talent and character to lead people! Many lies are wrapped in half-truths. My half-truth was not knowing the character of the Father and not recognizing that real leadership only comes through being a servant.

At one of the lowest points in my life, I traveled to Muslim-controlled Northern Sudan. In the darkest depths of my despair, approximately fifty Christian brothers and sisters surrounded me in a circle of love, in an empty field, and prayed for my wife's physical healing. It is not an exaggeration to say that I was touched to the core of my being by their servant-like desire to help my family and me in our hour of need. Although they had few possessions and nothing to offer beyond their love, concern, and prayers, it was enough—and one of the most humbling events I have experienced.

The story of Israel and its occupation of the Promised Land reminds me of my life. Clear vision (go and possess the land), difficult circumstances (giants), and questionable resolve by most to get the job done (with the exception of Joshua and Caleb). For the nation of Israel, additional time in the wilderness was required because of disobedience and the need for an attitude adjustment; however, victory eventually awaited those who stayed true to the Lord's instruction—even though a generation had to pass. This book tells the story of my Jericho March: from a promise to occupation, with wilderness in between; a journey that has spanned my lifetime. Unfortunately, it has taken that lifetime for God to awaken servanthood in me. Who wants to be weak? Who wants to be vulnerable? Those were things I always felt I could control. I did not realize that through my weakness, He is always made stronger. Through my vulnerability, toward both God and those around me, new levels of intimacy and heightened levels of leadership are achieved. It is only through serving that one can truly lead.

This is my story. I have tried to tell it in a way that respects the privacy* of my family. It is clear, however, that those who are the most important to me have played a prominent role in the events of this life, so they are often mentioned in these pages. I hope that my words adequately demonstrate the deep love and respect I have for each one of them. This account of my journey to servanthood is intended to encourage you, the reader. I have made a lot of mistakes along the way, but—thanks be to God—I am coming to recognize His intended destination for me.

* Out of respect for privacy and security concerns, some names have been changed.

CHAPTER ONE
SPIES IN A FOREIGN LAND

It was a cold morning in March of 1989, and the Hungarian/ Romanian border at Nadlac loomed less than five kilometers ahead of us. I pulled over to the side of the road, as was my custom when I was embarking on a mission of this nature, to commit to the Lord what would take place in the next several hours.

The crisp, cold morning air felt refreshing as I stepped out of the driver's seat of our silver Nissan. Already a veteran of numerous smuggling missions into Romania, I tried to convince myself that this was just another routine trip. Deep down, however, I knew that this assignment was different.

The mission organization that I worked with, Mission Possible, had just had one of its most experienced smugglers retire. He had been my partner, and his leadership and experience had taught me much over the previous twelve months. It was in this moment that I realized how much I had always depended on him.

To make matters worse, our key contact in Romania, who was the heart and soul of our smuggling operation, had just escaped the country. He had left behind an inexperienced replacement to carry on the work of coordinating our covert deliveries. This would be one of my first trips to "break him in," and I knew that the potential for disaster was great.

It was in these circumstances that I stepped into my first attempt at leadership. I had recently been put in charge of our organization's smuggling operations, and I could not help but feel less than capable of carrying the weight of responsibility that had been thrust upon me. Looking back, I recognize that too much authority at too young of an age certainly helped set me up to adopt a leadership style that emphasized influence and power over servanthood.

My partner for this trip was a supporter of our ministry. Don was a pleasant man, but the fact that he had never before traveled to Eastern Europe gave me the feeling that I was alone in this enterprise.

I did, however, have confidence in our vehicle. Having traveled over Eastern European borders more than forty times without being compromised, the Nissan provided us a better than average chance of crossing the frontier successfully. I also recognized, however, that the car's previously successful missions posed a problem. Because the all-terrain vehicle was so successful at crossing these borders, it had been used more times than was normally safe. While relatively few of the borders that we crossed in the 1980s had computers to check the frequency of the visits of a specific vehicle or passenger, the danger of a border guard recognizing the Nissan (which would happen to me almost six months later) was always present.

While Eastern European border crossings had not yet entered the computer age, Mission Possible had accomplished this several years earlier. The Mission Possible team used technology to document each vehicle and staff member's travel records. The organization tracked which borders had been crossed and how often, the color of the vehicle used, its license plate number, etc. Every precaution was taken to ensure that neither a vehicle nor its occupants would be recognized or put at greater risk than necessary. However, the closer I got to the actual border, the less confident I was in our man-centered methods of avoiding detection. That is why this final stop before the Romanian border was so important.

The Nissan's one and only secret compartment contained over two hundred assorted pieces of Christian literature, the majority of which were Romanian New Testaments and children's Bibles. These books were destined to reach the northernmost corner of Romania—Moldavia. While this shipment was rather small in quantity, it was worth its weight in gold to many Moldavian believers because of the lack of any form of Christian literature in this region.

One final check of the vehicle proved that we were at least physically ready to cross the frontier. Spiritually, however, I was not quite so sure.

As Don and I concluded our prayer, we took advantage of this last opportunity to stretch our legs before traveling on to the border. The contrast in our mood from the previous day's journey along the route to Romania was stark. We got back in the Nissan for the remaining five-kilometer drive, and the once talkative, exciting atmosphere that had been prevalent now gave way to a more somber and introspective climate. Situations such as the one in which we found ourselves gave new meaning to 1 Thessalonians 5:17 that directs us to "pray continually."

Up ahead, the Nadlac border loomed. I slowed the Nissan as we approached the Hungarian side of the crossing.

Having experienced the early winds of reform almost one year previously, Hungary had significantly loosened its border-crossing inspections. This was a welcome change for those of us who often had to travel through Hungary to get to a more hostile nation.

The crossing went without complications. We waited in a short line for the perfunctory "once over" of our vehicle and belongings by customs officials. Our passports were stamped, and we were allowed to continue on our way. The young soldier manning the blockade raised the barrier, permitting us to drive from Hungarian territory into no man's land—the three-hundred-meter stretch that separated the two frontiers.

Now, the Romanian guard towers were close enough that we could see the watchmen perched upon their crow's nests with their rifles and binoculars in hand.

A young soldier standing in the roadway ahead of us motioned for our vehicle to drive through the disinfectant trap to "decontaminate" our vehicle before it touched Romanian soil. The murky color of the trap's contents caused me to suspect that it was filled with nothing more than that month's accumulated rainfall.

As we approached the dilapidated buildings that served as Nadlac's customs outpost, vehicles were divided into two lanes. One was for Westerners, and one was for Eastern Europeans. It was obvious which lane was which. The distinction between the Romanian-made Dachas and Russian Ladas, both resembling rolling tin cans, and the Mercedes and Audis would be apparent even to a child.

There were about five cars in front of us as we settled in for what could be a wait of anywhere from one to six hours, depending on the mood of the officials making the inspections in front of us.

Each car ahead of us was systematically searched, and minutes ticked into hours of waiting. Because we were in line behind several other vehicles, it allowed us the unnerving vantage point of watching as each vehicle was subjected to a more-than-thorough search of its contents.

As car after car unloaded its cargo onto the tables provided for just such an inspection, the realization began to sink in that we would be next.

Our passports had already been taken, and visa fees had been paid in anticipation of being allowed to enter the country. Customs officials, however, held our passports until one final formality was taken care of—the inspection of our car and belongings.

The last car in front of us repacked their belongings and then received their clearance to enter Romania. We were motioned to drive forward to the lowered barrier, which was the only thing now separating us from entering the country.

"Take everything out of your car," a customs officer in a grey, tattered uniform barked to us as he approached my driver's side window. He had just exited his lair inside of the customs building.

Don and I quickly jumped out and lowered the Nissan's tailgate to comply with the order. The official walked around the vehicle and inspected it with great curiosity.

We began to stack the enormous amount of contents of the Nissan on the inspection table. The customs guard approached me and demanded that I open the hood. I immediately complied and then returned to unpacking. I watched him from the corner of my eye as he began his inspection.

I typically traveled with lots of hard-to-get fresh fruits that I would give to our various contacts in Romania. Bananas were especially difficult to keep fresh if I traveled in the cold winter months. By the time we got them in the country, they usually resembled what a grocer would throw away.

On this particular trip, I was especially loaded down. Several months earlier, I had agreed to cooperate with a Baptist pastor in Arad, who wanted to evangelize several Romanian orphanages. I was to bring with me the contents for one hundred and fifty packets that would include Western items such as gum, candy, pens, combs, brushes, hair clips, and other small trinkets. These packets would then be assembled by Baptist believers who would, in turn, and at great personal risk, give them out to Romanian orphans. The packets, containing unheard of items for the orphans, would be the avenue through which the Gospel could be shared one-on-one with each child.

Since this project was not a top priority for our organization (Christian literature and Bibles got first priority in our secret compartment space), I could not use our secret compartment to bring these items into the country. That meant that several trips had been necessary to avoid being noticed because of the large amounts of brushes, combs, and the like that we were transporting. This was the last of several loads that would allow the Christians in Arad to distribute the packets by Easter. Seeing the contents of the Nissan piled up on the customs table, however, I began to wonder if I had gone a little overboard with my purchases.

Having been well-briefed on conduct and what to expect at the border, and despite the aggressive nature of our particular border agent, Don seemed to maintain his composure well.

In pre-trip briefings, I would usually exaggerate the negative side of what one might possibly experience on a smuggling mission. I assumed that if I prepared my traveling companion for the worst, they could then be pleasantly surprised when the trip's outcome was positive.

I hoped that our hours of discussions as to what to expect and what to say or not say if our content was discovered had made an impact on Don. It was standard Mission Possible procedure not to divulge the details of a trip that involved crossing the Romanian border, including where the literature was hidden in the vehicle, to an inexperienced traveling companion. This was to ensure protection for everyone involved in the mission in the event that my partner cracked under the pressure of an interrogation. This trip was no exception.

In my experience, if a smuggler and his traveling companion were caught, they would usually be separated for interrogation. Once the interrogation started, the goal would be to find out where the shipment of Bibles was going in-country. There was not much that the Romanian government could do to stop people from attempting to smuggle Bibles into Romania, but they could certainly make life difficult for the ones receiving the Bibles. This could even mean imprisonment; therefore, the less information that my traveling partner knew, the better.

At the conclusion of an interrogation and inspection where contraband was found, the most common outcome was typically the confiscation of the vehicle and the guilty parties being refused entry into the country.

Our inspector seemed preoccupied with the diesel motor of our Nissan, and after numerous minutes of investigation, he approached our mountain of food and clothing piled alongside the car for inspection. He nonchalantly began to rifle through our belongings, and he also started the questioning.

"Why are you here?"

"I am a travel guide showing my friend around Romania," I replied, pointing to Don.

"Where are you going?" he sternly asked. I explained that we were going to tour several major cities in Romania.

Without further hesitation, he inquired, "Do you have guns, drugs, pornographic materials, or Bibles?" Without blinking, I looked him straight in the eyes. In a non-compromising voice, I responded simply, "No."

I certainly believe that it is unethical to lie, yet I have been convinced, through years of seeing God's miraculous provision on Eastern European borders and my own personal study of God's Word, that deception is not an unforgivable sin. The Bible is full of deceptive events that eventually worked for God's glory. In Jericho, Rahab, the prostitute hid the Israelites in order to evade detection. In Damascus, Paul escaped from the hands of King Aretas and his governor by being lowered from the city wall in a basket.

While God certainly can work in miraculous ways to make seeing eyes blind, those of us who made Bible smuggling a monthly occupation were often confronted with the straightforward and simple question: "Do you have Bibles?" If my answer had been "yes" (as colleagues in the past had done) without divine intervention, the consequences would have been confiscation of the literature and the vehicle, and an interrogation that most likely would have meant endangering the lives of our in-country contacts. Mission Possible, as a smuggling organization, would also have been compromised.

When I started my career as a Bible smuggler, I made the decision that I would not compromise the security of the Lord's servants (my brothers and sisters in Christ) and their families, just as I would not betray my family sleeping in the next room should a murderer break in and demand to know where they were. Many might have a problem telling such a lie on a consistent basis, but I slept undisturbed with my decision.

As someone who has lied numerous times, regardless of whether the circumstances seemed justifiable, I am a liar. And, "Thou shalt not lie" is a commandment I have broken. I have laid this before the Lord and have asked for His forgiveness.

Without any further questions, the customs official turned his attention back to the Nissan. Although he had searched through every single box, parcel, and suitcase that we had, he never seemed to notice the peculiar items for children that two grown men were carrying with them on their travels!

Our customs agent summoned a mechanic to begin investigating the underside of the Nissan as he proceeded from front to rear, knocking on the vehicle's outer walls and listening for even the most minor of discrepancies in sound.

Another agent was thoroughly investigating the Nissan's uncharacteristically large heating unit. Although it had absolutely nothing to do with where our literature was hidden, its large protruding size greatly interested our examiners.

After some time of investigation, convinced that if we had anything hidden, it must be somewhere else, they turned their attention toward the rear of the vehicle.

After half an hour of looking over our car, the examiners approached the main Bible storage compartment in the rear. Unbeknownst to everyone, including Don, our guards were about to examine the area that contained the floor entrance to the Nissan's secret compartment. It was what we referred to as "the system."

The guards began to probe the cargo bay, and I was immediately taken aback by what seemed to me to be an incredible resolve on the part of our guard to exhaustively search this car. I knew that, should his sole attention remain on the cargo area for too much longer, our chances of leaving this border undetected were slim.

Inwardly, I wondered exactly what incentive our enthusiastic friend might have for his thorough search. Often the Romanian government rewarded customs officials very well for finding hidden contraband. Was our agent in serious need of a bonus?

My heart began to pound, and my mind raced as the officer began inspecting the exact location of the system's trigger mechanism. The trigger was the key to the entire system.

While normally it took up to half an hour under favorable conditions to open the compartment, once the trigger was discovered, it was as simple as connecting the dots and following the next logical steps necessary to gain full entrance.

I wanted to look away and not to watch as this stranger probed so inquisitively what I had prayed would remain hidden from him. But I couldn't look away. It was as if I was frozen in time and destined to witness, in what felt like slow motion, the discovery of our hidden shipment of God's Word.

At this moment, I sent one final silent plea to the Lord. "Father, protect us and your vehicle!" There was no time for more. Immediately, as that final prayer was uttered via the Holy Spirit inside of me, the guard's focus shifted from the floor of the cargo bay to the Nissan's tailgate.

Heaving an inward sigh of relief, I knew that we were not out of the woods yet. This guard's tenacity would not allow him to give up until either he had found something or he was absolutely sure that there was nothing to find. While his focus might have momentarily shifted to the tailgate, I knew that he was not yet finished. Six very interesting bolts on the tailgate's inside surface would now entertain our friend for the next several minutes.

This was the moment for which I had prayed and so often had witnessed as I crossed border after border: the moment of God's miraculous intervention. In over six years and more than fifty different smuggling operations that had been conducted via this vehicle, what was about to happen had never occurred before, nor would it ever be repeated.

As my faith in God's provision for us began to show signs of stress fatigue, so, too, did the metal tailgate hinge on the Nissan.

As the guard closed and reopened the tailgate in the process of his examination, the metal arm hinge bent as if it were rubber. It moved in a horizontal rather than a vertical direction as it was designed. The end result was what appeared to be the total destruction of my tailgate's ability to open and close, and all by the hands of our inquisitive customs official.

Recognizing God's direct intervention on our behalf, I knew exactly how to proceed.

"What have you done to my car?" I shouted. "Look at it! It is totally wrecked!" The customs guard, momentarily shocked by my outburst, slowly began to realize what it was that he had just done. "Do you know how much this is going to cost to have repaired?" I demanded. "At least three hundred dollars," I replied, not waiting for his response. "I am not leaving this border until you've paid me in cash, U.S. dollars, for the damage you've done to my car," I firmly declared.

The look of shock on the custom official's face turned to a look of horror. Realizing that he was now in serious trouble with the threat of having to pay me over six months of his wages, he immediately forgot all about the search that had been underway. He shifted his concentration to trying to convince me that, "We can fix this."

I knew that the tide had now turned. The Lord had given us a way out of what had just moments before seemed to have been an impossible situation. All that was left for me to do was to play this game out to its predetermined conclusion. The reality that the Lord had already won was evident.

I went to the front of the Nissan and pulled out the tool kit that was under the back seat. As I returned to the tailgate with tools in hand, several guards were now attempting to show me that the damage was really not that serious. After ten minutes of hammering, prying, and bending, my elated customs friends now pronounced the tailgate "fixed." They could tell, though, by the look on my face that I was anything but happy about what had just transpired, including the fruits of their labor.

With the tailgate now operable, what I had hoped would happen as a result of this little incident became a reality. The guards were so anxious to get us out of there and on our way that the only thing hindering us from leaving immediately was the amount of time that it took us to re-pack the Nissan.

Vehicle loaded and passports in hand, the guards—now all smiles—quickly waved us onward. As the young soldier raised the barricade just high enough to allow the Nissan to slip underneath, the elation of having made it once again, with the Lord's help, made me want to shout for joy.

As our car slowly pulled out onto the narrow two-lane road, which led us to our first stop, the border city of Arad, the excitement of having crossed the border successfully once again was combined with a prayer of thanksgiving to God for His watchful care.

Don still had no idea of exactly how close we had come to being discovered. The next several minutes were spent excitedly discussing what had just transpired. In this instance, Don's previous ignorance of where the literature had been hidden was most certainly bliss.

As the first propaganda sign appeared along the roadside, "Long live Nicolae Ceausescu and the Communist Party of Romania," I knew that, despite our successful crossing, the real work was just beginning.

Just as Israel had sent Caleb and Joshua into the land of Canaan to scout it out, I also hoped that I would be returning with a good report. We were most definitely spies in a foreign land.

CHAPTER TWO
A CALL TO SERVICE

The year 1974 was a year of change for my family. My father, Ralph Mann, was a successful lawyer who was practicing as the City Attorney for Denton, Texas. I was ten years old, and my two brothers, Jim and Mark, were five and four. The three of us were too young to realize what a significant year this would be in the course of our family's history.

Both my parents had been praying earnestly for quite some time for the Lord's direction in their lives. Although Dad had been happy in the legal profession, he had begun to question whether or not God was pleased with what he was doing for a living.

It was at this time that my parents were exposed to the needs of Eastern Europe. While visiting a backyard Bible study, a guest speaker scorched the hearts of my parents with his stories of needy Russian believers and the oppression that was a part of their daily lives. My parents left the meeting that night asking the Lord if this might be the direction in which He was calling them.

Through numerous acts of confirmation, the Lord made it clear to both Mom and Dad that they were, with their three small children, to step out in faith and enter the uncertain world of fulltime Christian ministry to Eastern Europe. It was at this point that Dad set aside his lifelong ambitions in the legal field to follow that greater call, which was the voice of the Shepherd saying, "Follow Me."

And thus, the ministry of *Mission Possible* was born. Dad set his hand to the plow from his spacious new office in the playroom of our house. Having just a handful of names for a mailing list and no operating funds, the Lord honored my father's obedience and prospered *Mission Possible* over the years.

While not able to understand the change that took place spiritually in the lives of my parents, I did understand the economic change that was forced upon our family—and I didn't like it. We had never experienced a lavish lifestyle growing up, but money had never seemed to be a problem. The change in routine that we now experienced was apparent, even to a young boy of ten.

Vacations, which were previously filled with lots of fun and nice hotels, now consisted of church meetings and speaking engagements for Dad, with an occasional trip on the side to the local tourist attraction. It would not be until my adult years that I would appreciate all of the fascinating locations I was privileged to visit with Mom and Dad when I was young.

I remember sitting in meeting after meeting with my family, often being able to predict the next story that Dad would tell. My brothers and I memorized word for word the video tape of Eastern Europe that Dad would show. It became the brunt of many a family joke.

Mission Possible's mailout crew, which was responsible for the monthly mailings of its newsletter to an ever-increasing database, consisted of Mom and the three of us boys. An occasional pizza would be necessary to keep the often-discontented workers from striking. As the years went on, and as our entire family became more involved in the ministry to Eastern Europe, I longed to separate myself from it.

Our family had always been active in the Southern Baptist denomination. I made a profession of faith in Jesus Christ as my Lord and Savior at the age of seven. It was a sincere act and was one that established a relationship between the Lord and me. This decision would help carry me through my teenage years.

Junior high and high school were filled with the normal concerns of a teenage boy: sports, first date, driver's license, studies, and the like. Each, of course, seemed to be unprecedented in the scope of human history.

Despite the occasional stumbling that is common to any teenager, my relationship with the Lord remained strong. Although my faith in Christ was steadfast, my commitment to follow His will for my life was not.

By the end of my time in high school, I carried no bitterness or resentment regarding Dad's career change. I still could not understand, however, how someone could give up so much that they had worked so hard to achieve. I knew that I would follow my own course in life. All of those things that Dad had given up would someday be mine. I was determined to be a lawyer, but unlike Dad, my ambitions would not be derailed.

In the summer of 1982, our family traveled to Europe to "vacation in Romania." This was what we told the Romanian guards as we crossed their border with more than two thousand pieces of Christian literature hidden in the walls of our van. Although everything went without a hitch, it certainly was not one of the highlights of my life. I remember that my impression of communist Romania was that anyone could make the mistake of visiting this country once, but only a real fool would go back a second time. That experience only strengthened my resolve to stay as far away from Eastern Europe as possible. I returned home excited to be an American and ready to get on with the rest of my life.

While I did well in school academically, I did not enjoy it much. I didn't develop a real preference as to which university I wanted to attend. I applied to several, but I was not excited about any.

A few years earlier on one of our family's numerous *Mission Possible* trips, Mom and Dad drove us through the campus of Oral Roberts University in Tulsa, Oklahoma. I barely remember the experience, but it must have made a lasting impression on my parents. When the time came for me to choose a school, both Mom and Dad were determined that I at least consider ORU.

So, in light of no other exciting prospects, I did consider it. I even visited the campus, but I returned home still as uncommitted as ever to any one school in particular. As the time to make a final decision inched its way closer, my parents' encouragement led me to lean toward ORU. Since Mom and Dad had committed to paying for my studies and there wasn't another school that I was excited to attend, I made up my mind to head toward Tulsa in the fall. Dad and

I agreed that once I started at ORU, I would try it for at least a year. If at the end of that time I was not happy, then I could transfer to the school of my choice, within their budget of course.

I didn't sleep at all the night before Mom was to drive me to Oklahoma. I remember lying in bed awake, thinking that from this point on in my life nothing would be the same. Little did I know how correct I was. The Lord would especially use this next year to bring me closer to Him.

My first weeks at ORU were filled with the stress of registration and beginning classes in a totally new environment. The reality of being on my own also hit hard. As I finally began to make new friends and settle into a routine, the cloud of fear that had hung over those first few weeks gave way to the sunshine of independence.

I began to enjoy my classes and newfound friends. However, as the months went on, there was something about the school that disturbed my comfort zone. Through chapel services and dormitory floor devotionals, I felt as if I was being asked to demonstrate a deeper commitment to Jesus Christ than I had actually experienced. Also, there were a few individuals on my floor who made me feel extremely uncomfortable about myself and my relationship with God. One of these young men was named Steve Elliott, our wing Chaplain. The other, Mike Jeffries, would soon become my roommate and best friend.

At first, Steve was especially bothersome. His example of Christ-like servanthood almost made me sick. I grew tired of returning to my dorm room after a long day of work and classes to find my bed perfectly made and everything neat and tidy (in stark contrast to how I had left things only a few hours earlier). Although Steve wasn't my roommate, he would just decide on his own to come into my room and clean it up for me. "Didn't this guy have anything better to do with his time?" I often asked myself.

Then, there was Mike. Mike really began to drive me crazy with his generosity. I can't count the number of times during my four years at ORU that Mike would treat me to dinner, a movie, or a concert. None of us had any money, but Mike worked several part-time jobs on the side to earn a little extra. My friends and I would see to it that his "little extra" was always gone by month's end. Mike didn't use his money to buy friends—he didn't need to do that—but his spirit of giving was obvious. I had never experienced this before, and the Judas Iscariot in me was deeply troubled by his example.

The pressure I felt, at least at first, was unquestionably a result of the Holy Spirit using these men to point out problems in my spiritual walk. No one ever banged me over the head and yelled, "Repent, sinner!" Rather, the gentle Spirit of God tugged at my heart strings and called me closer to Him.

By the end of November that first semester, I couldn't take anymore. I had come to the realization that for me there were only two options: the first was giving in to the movement of the Holy Spirit in my life, and the second was running away as fast as I could go. Since I could not allow this "fanatic thing," as I termed it, to destroy my plans for the future, I had no other choice than to leave ORU as quickly as possible. I would not return for a second semester. I was able to hold on, or should I say, "fight off the Spirit," until Christmas break. Driving home, I had a good feeling knowing that I would never again be thrust into that spiritual pressure cooker. Now all I had to do was inform Mom and Dad of my decision.

As I broached the subject with Dad, I was shocked by his response. He immediately reminded me of our agreement for a one-year trial period at ORU. But couldn't he see how unhappy I was there? I tried my best to convince him to forget our agreement, but he remained steadfast.

I was devastated. Although I certainly remembered our verbal contract, I never thought that he would hold me to it once I explained to him how miserable ORU made me. Now I was facing the real prospect of having to return there for a second semester! The thought was enough to make me sick.

Christmas break was ruined for me. Over the course of the holidays, I continued to try to convince Dad of his mistake. As my time at home drew to a close, I was confronted with the reality that I had to return to the school from which I had literally fled just weeks previously. The last few days of vacation were spent resigning myself to the fact that I was going back.

The return drive to Tulsa gave me lots of time for inward reflection. Something inside of me was beginning to give way. It was as if I no longer had the willpower to continue to resist God. Despite all of my best efforts to keep God locked in my spiritual closet, only bringing Him out when I felt it appropriate, He continued to show me that this was not enough for Him. Why did God have to have everything? Wasn't I allowed to have any desires or dreams of my own? These questions continued to torment me. But most frightening of all was that I was beginning to feel like I knew the answers to my own questions. The success, prosperity, and purpose in life that I longed for could only be achieved through total surrender to Christ. Deep down, I knew what was required of me. While I wasn't quite ready to surrender, God was making progress.

The first few weeks of January 1984 were the most pivotal in my life. I began to contemplate this step of turning over to the Lord absolutely everything I had and was as a person. I also began to ask God bold new questions. Could I really trust Him to provide for me? Did He really care more about me than I cared about myself? It was so hard to believe, but still that gentle tug of the Spirit kept assuring me that it was true.

During these days, I also dared to open up to Steve. I told him about the spiritual turmoil that I was experiencing. He listened but didn't push me. He must have sensed that the Holy Spirit was in the process of doing something big with me, and God didn't need his help. If these were Steve's thoughts, then he certainly was correct.

Sunday, January 22, 1984 was the day that the Lord would finally have His way in my life. As I sat in church that morning, the pastor mentioned a special service that they were having that evening for those who wanted to give their lives completely to God. Although I normally studied for Monday morning exams on Sunday night, I knew that God was going to use this service to touch me. The anticipation was so great that it was hard for me to go about my normal Sunday activities. In fact, Steve later told me that he knew God was going to work in my life that evening. The Holy Spirit had brought me exactly to this point. I was now open and ready to first surrender and then to receive what the Lord had in store for me.

At that service, I experienced the power of the Holy Spirit like never before. I surrendered my life, in its entirety, to the Lord. "Use me as You will" was my prayer that evening. God responded by pouring out His Spirit in abundance upon me.

As I related to Steve the events of the previous evening, we established Proverbs 27:9 as a covenant Scripture. "Perfume and incense bring joy to the heart, and the pleasantness of one's friend springs from his earnest counsel." Both Steve and Mike would provide that counsel for me over the course of the next several years. Their love and Christ-like example would challenge me to new spiritual heights.

With my act of capitulation complete, Jesus Christ was now able to begin rebuilding the spiritual foundation of my life brick by brick. It would not be easy, and it would not happen overnight, but bit by bit my orientation shifted from self to Christ.

In addition to my part-time job and studies, I spent quite a bit of my free time that second semester with Mike and Steve. Over the course of the next five months, I grew spiritually by leaps and bounds. As the school year drew to a close, I had still not abandoned my ambitions of being an attorney; however, I was now asking the question, "Is this what You would have me do with my life, Lord?" That was a major step.

The change in me spiritually that last semester of my freshman year at ORU totally revised my opinion of the school. As final exams closed out the year that spring, I knew that I would be returning to finish both my degree and my spiritual quest.

But first there was to be a brief interruption to my academic life. My parents were planning to move with my two younger brothers to Europe to restructure *Mission Possible's* European operations. I decided to join them, which meant sitting out the first semester of the upcoming 1984/1985 school year. After a month of working to make a few extra dollars, we left for Vienna, Austria in June of 1984.

I used the next seven months to spend much time one-on-one with the Lord. After living a month with my family in Vienna and studying German, I headed off on my own to see Europe. Three months on the road gave me ample time to work on my relationship with the Lord. God really used this time to solidify the commitment I had made to Him that previous January.

In the meantime, my father relocated *Mission Possible's* center of operations for its covert activities in Eastern Europe to southern Germany. After gallivanting around the capitals of Europe, I spent my last few months and Christmas with my family in Bavaria, before I returned to ORU.

Mike and I had corresponded throughout the course of the fall semester, and we had decided to room together upon my return in January. I arrived back at ORU with a new sensitivity to the world and the lost and dying people in it. The Lord was in the first phase of placing on my heart a call to service.

Mike and I became steadfast friends that semester, and God used him to continue to transform my life.

With my parents continuing to live in Europe, I needed to find a place to call home during my summer break. I chose to travel back to Texas to stay with close friends of our family who had graciously agreed to put me up for the summer.

Work and summer school at the University of North Texas were the order of the day. I felt it was essential to make up several courses that I had missed during my semester's absence. Work was now a necessity to make ends meet and occupied the free hours that I was not in class.

I changed churches that summer and made many new friends who challenged me spiritually. This new environment kept me actively pursuing whatever it was that God might have in store for my life. I would not allow these summer months to create an environment where I slipped back into a state of apathy toward God.

But little did I know that a new "thorn in the flesh" would soon challenge my determination to stay the course in regard to my walk with the Lord.

Midway through the summer, I began to experience excruciating pains in my stomach. At first, I was sure that my periodic bouts of discomfort were no big deal. But as the pains continued to worsen in intensity and frequency, I wasn't so sure. After I consulted with both family and friends, I decided to be tested for an ulcer. I was shocked as the doctor diagnosed me as having a duodenal ulcer.

For some reason, I had always assumed that only stressed-out, middle-aged executives got ulcers. Here I was at the ripe old age of twenty popping ulcer medication as if it was candy to relieve the pain I was experiencing. Predictably, I began to ask, "Why me, Lord?"

As the summer wore on, my new circumstances somewhat diminished my spiritual zeal. More than ever I began to feel like I needed a sign from the Lord to prove to me that He was going to help me over this new physical speed bump.

And God did speak to me; however, I was unprepared for what He had to say.

Driving to work one afternoon, I experienced God's presence like never before. I was listening to the radio, with my thoughts concentrated on nothing in particular, when I heard what almost sounded like an audible voice.

The voice asked me, "Do you believe that the Bible is My Holy Word?" Surprised by what apparently was happening, I thought for a second about the question. It didn't take me long to respond with the answer, "Of course." The next question that was asked would change my outlook on Christianity forever. The voice responded, "Then why don't you do what it says?"

Stunned by this experience, I began to think about what the Lord was trying to tell me. I concluded that both my understanding and application of God's Word to my daily life were lacking. Thus, I started to study the Bible like never before. Drawing closer to God through the study of His Word would prove critical in helping me survive the next several years living with ulcer problems. The event that took place that summer afternoon on my way to work would remain a milestone as it related to my relationship with the Lord.

Once school began again in the fall, I felt impressed by the Lord to participate in ORU's summer mission program. Since Dad was involved in Eastern European mission work, I began to inquire both of *Mission Possible* and the ORU mission leadership team if there was interest in planning a short-term summer mission trip to Eastern Europe. I was excited to find out that both sides were very interested in the idea.

In the meantime, Steve had been praying about his involvement in this potential outreach and had come to the conclusion that he would join me if such a trip were to materialize. Both Steve and I were looking forward to the idea of spending the summer together on a mission trip.

As communication between ORU and *Mission Possible* intensified, two teams were established that were to go to Eastern Europe. One group would travel the Soviet Union for two months, while the other group would tour Hungary, Poland, Yugoslavia, Romania, and Bulgaria. Both teams would try to do as much work as possible with the local churches in these politically repressive countries. Evangelism was also a goal, but such activities would have to be limited due to the hostile religious climate in Eastern Europe and the Soviet Union.

When it came time for the ORU leadership to pick the members for each team, Steve and I requested that, if possible, we be placed on the same outreach. Several days later we were both called into the mission office and informed that they would like for both Steve and I to be team leaders—of separate teams. We had not counted on this happening. It took us both several days of prayer and discussion before we agreed with the mission department's recommendation. Even though we began to get excited about the possibilities of the two-team concept, the disappointment of knowing that we would not be traveling together remained.

Everything that school year seemed to focus on our upcoming summer mission trips. Time seemed to fly by as I supplemented my already busy schedule of school and work with team mission meetings. I would lead a team to the

Soviet Union while Steve would lead his team to the other Eastern European countries. The amount of preparation needed seemed endless. Planning included everything from visas to travel logistics. Coordinating a trip to Soviet Russia was a daunting task.

As the end of the school year drew near, the anticipation for both of our trips reached a crescendo. My team's departure was less than a month away and all of our preparations, except for our visas, were complete. Our travel agent continued to reassure us that this last-minute waiting was normal, and that our visas should be approved any day. We found ourselves faced with no other option but to wait.

On the 26th of April 1986, I returned to my dorm room just in time to watch the national evening news. Little did I know that the lead story that night would end up disrupting the lives of millions, as well as over ten months of careful planning and preparation that my team and I had completed. The event that took place that day caused such worldwide fear that one word is enough to make most people recollect the scope of its tragedy—Chernobyl.

I watched in horror as those first reports came in, and a sinking feeling prepared me for the worst. As Chernobyl spewed its nuclear fallout over thousands of kilometers, the political fallout was to reach as far as my tiny dorm room in Tulsa, Oklahoma.

Our team's itinerary was to take us through the Ukrainian capital of Kiev three times, and unfortunately for us, that was just a stone's throw away from the burning nuclear reactor.

We continued to make preparations to travel those next few weeks following the disaster. It was difficult, however, to get any real answers as to the full extent of the nuclear contamination. Of course, the Soviets weren't saying anything in an attempt to downplay the tragedy. Therefore, as far as we knew, our visas were still being processed. The added stress that this new development placed on my team members was incredible. It also did not help my ulcer.

On the day before we were scheduled to leave, we still had received no word in regard to our visas. Plane tickets had already been purchased. My team members were preparing to catch flights out the next morning for our rendezvous in New York before proceeding together to Moscow. One of my team members, Jay Shennum, had already left his hometown and was waiting in a hotel room in Kansas City in anticipation of his early morning flight the next day.

By now, our travel agent had sent a personal envoy to the Soviet consulate in New York to secure our visas. I sat nervously by the phone all evening waiting for the good news that would never come.

At approximately eight p.m., I received the call that we would not be traveling in the immediate future. While the Soviets had not denied us visas, they did refuse to issue them to us at the present time. The only words of explanation were, "Not now. Maybe in a week."

What followed was one of the most unpleasant experiences I have faced. I was required to call all of my team members to inform them that the trip for which we had prepared numerous months was not going to take place. Some of them were out making last minute trip purchases. Leaving messages on their answering machines made it even harder. The telephone call to Jay, who was alone in his Kansas City hotel room, was the most difficult of them all.

The trip was not officially called off until two weeks later. At that point, the logistics became impossible to manage, with the uncertainty of visas as much a problem as ever. Sensing my team members needed to be able to salvage their summer plans, we reluctantly gave up on our dream.

Steve's team was a different story. Despite the fact that radioactive fallout had landed on most of Eastern Europe, Steve's team felt that the potential risks to them for such a short period of time were minimal. Nor was it a problem for them to get visas, many of which they already had in their possession. Since Steve's group was scheduled to leave several weeks after our planned departure, Steve asked me if I would like to join them as a member of their team. After praying about this for a few days, I decided that it was not the right thing for me to do in light of the disappointment that my team had just experienced. Although I certainly would have relished going, I reluctantly declined the invitation. Disappointed beyond words, it now looked as if my destiny was another summer of work and ulcer medication. It would take me almost a year to secure refunds that I had negotiated with travel agents and to pay back donors who had contributed to our now scrapped mission trip. A year later, as more ORU students prepared to go on summer outreaches, I was still busy dealing with the finances of the previous year's failed Soviet trip.

A few months before Steve's team departed, I was invited to join him and his crew on a Saturday afternoon rock climbing outing. I noticed a beautiful young woman on his team named Michelle, and that first look made a lasting impression. With their mission trip just around the corner, I put my interest in Michelle on hold for the time being.

The summer of 1986 was long, and returning to school in the fall looked so good to me. One of the first social events that I was invited to attend was a party hosted by Steve for his Eastern European team members. Excited to hear more about their trip and their experiences, I awaited the day of the party with much anticipation. When I arrived at Steve's parents' home, one of the first guests that I noticed was Michelle.

Having been overwhelmed by my own misfortunes that summer, I had almost forgotten the beautiful young lady who had so intrigued me only months earlier. But now as I spent another afternoon in her presence, those emotions returned like a flood.

As classes got underway, to my great pleasure I noticed that Michelle was in attendance at one of my humanities lectures. I wasted little time trying to befriend her, and I immediately began to contemplate the best way to go about asking her out on a date. Several lectures elapsed, and I failed to exploit some missed opportunities. Finally, my nerve was up. As I escorted Michelle back to her dorm one afternoon, she agreed to go out with me. I was elated.

Michelle and I began to see more and more of each other over the course of the remaining months of 1986. By Christmas, I was convinced that Michelle was the woman of my dreams. Convincing Michelle of my unbeatable merits was a little more difficult.

We continued to date that next spring, and our hearts grew closer as we spent more of our free hours together.

Ulcers continued to be a problem for me. As I began to sense that God might be calling me into full-time ministry, I was still mystified by my chronic illness. Looking back on those months, I am amazed that Michelle stood by my side through what was a very sickly physical state for a courtship.

As spring turned into summer, Michelle and I continued to date long distance via telephone and an occasional visit. We both prepared to return to ORU in the fall of 1987. This would be my final semester and Michelle's junior year, and we realized that the next few months would be a defining period in our relationship.

Sensing God's calling on my life more clearly now, I seriously began to consider serving with *Mission Possible* as a Bible courier once school was complete. While I was beginning to feel more comfortable understanding God's will for my life, a new obstacle developed to keep me from committing to overseas mission work. It was the fear of losing my relationship with Michelle.

If I agreed to go with *Mission Possible*, I would be required to sign a two-year commitment. I would be stationed in Germany for the entire two-year period. No return trips to the U.S. would be allowed until my furlough at the conclusion of my contract.

When Michelle graduated, which was still a year away, she would be required to take a job in the public accounting field for at least a year in order to obtain her Certified Public Accountant credentials. I felt certain that such a separation of both distance and time would be the death blow to our relationship. The prospects of a minimum absence of two years from her seemed like an eternity to me. I could not muster up the faith to place these new circumstances in the hands of my heavenly Father.

During my closing days of academia, I began contemplating other job options that would keep me in Tulsa close to Michelle. It was easy for me to rationalize why it would be best for me to stay close to home, including getting some much-needed cash in my pocket. I imagined that after her completion of school and her year in the accounting industry, being madly in love, we would marry and contemplate life on the mission field. It made such perfect sense.

Job opportunities were there for me, but the only problem was that they brought with them little peace to my spirit. The more I considered not going on the mission field, the more miserable I became. Through much prayer and discussion with Michelle and other trusted friends, I began to realize that the best place a child of God can be is in the center of His will. Although my faith was truly no larger than the size of a mustard seed, I summoned the courage to commit myself to God's service in Eastern Europe. The fear had not left me; however, I had taken my first major step on what would be a life-changing journey.

The last few months of 1987 were a wonderful time for Michelle and me as we took advantage of every opportunity to be together. As school concluded for me that December, Michelle and I committed to trying to maintain the relationship. I left the ORU campus for the last time as a student and drove back home. On that drive, I had an unwanted companion—fear. Specifically, the fear of losing the one I loved.

Over the course of the first eight months of 1988, I was required by *Mission Possible* to raise the monthly income that I needed to sustain me on the mission field from donors.

During this time, I was able to make numerous weekend visits to Tulsa to see Michelle. Although we had wonderful times together on each trip, it was obvious that the two years ahead of us would be much different from our days together at ORU.

As the deadline for my overseas departure drew closer, my persisting ulcer problems gave me great cause for alarm. Not only had I offered up to God the woman I wanted to marry, but now I was headed into what I considered one of the most stress-filled occupations anyone could imagine with an ulcer problem! I was having a very difficult time trying to figure out God's logic in all of this.

Through it all, however, the call to service remained strong. As I sat alone in a Subway deli two days before my departure, ulcer flair-up and all, an overwhelming peace came upon me. I somehow knew that at this point, remaining true to the call was everything.

It was all on the table now. Everything I had to offer was now before the Lord. It was all laid at His feet to do with as He saw fit. He knew my pain, my needs, and my concerns, and He had grasp of the big picture. In contrast, all I had were the promises of God's Word.

As I stepped onto my plane bound for Europe, I did not look back. It was now time to keep my eyes focused straight ahead and watch to see what the Lord would do.

CHAPTER THREE
A GOOD REPORT

As our Nissan began to put some miles between ourselves and the Romanian Border, I thought about my previous life in school, together with Michelle, before becoming a Bible smuggler. Those days seemed a distant memory now, far in the rearview mirror. God equips those He calls, but I was not sure my years in academia at ORU had prepared me for what I was now experiencing.

Both Don and I were glad that we had left the vicinity of the frontier. The level of tension in the vehicle lowered substantially. Ahead was the final checkpoint before we entered the interior of Romania, and it was manned only by two soldiers. Since these soldiers' job was primarily to stop unauthorized persons from approaching the border crossing into Hungary, it was likely that they would be more concerned with traffic that was traveling in the opposite direction. As often had been the case, a mere slowing of our vehicle and a wave of our passports allowed us to continue uninterrupted. We now had approximately fifteen kilometers to travel before we reached Arad, our first destination.

I started to think of the work that still needed to be completed before the day was done, and I again asked the Lord for His help to accomplish it all. Our vehicle was what we described in smuggling vernacular as "hot," meaning we were still very much in danger due to the literature inside the Nissan's secret compartment. Standard protocol was to take care of this problem as quickly as possible.

Our schedule would be tight. Since our border crossing was near the city of Arad, the destination of our materials that were needed for the orphanage evangelism project, that would be our first stop. We would then be required to travel north an additional 100 kilometers to the city of Oradea. We were to arrive before nightfall so that we would not be required to travel on Romania's dangerous thoroughfares after dark. One never knew when an unlit horse-drawn cart would appear on the pitch-black road ahead of you and cause a collision. Several years earlier, a fellow smuggler had been imprisoned for hitting a drunk member of the military at night. Because of this, I was careful to be finished with my driving by sundown.

Once in Oradea, we would wait for nightfall before establishing contact with those who would facilitate the unloading of the vehicle.

This day, March 16, 1989, was dreary and overcast. The weather in Romania so often seemed to reflect the cloud of oppression that I felt hung over the country. The dictatorship of Nicolae Ceausescu had certainly taken its toll on Romania. Strapped with an astronomical debt to Western nations, Ceausescu, at the expense of the Romanian people, had made the arbitrary decision to repay the debt in full in a matter of a few years.

Virtually everything that had any value was exported to the West in his drive for hard currency (what the Romanians called Valuta). Every day in Western Europe, scores of Romanian trucks could be seen traveling to any destination that would pay them hard currency for their products and natural resources. This meant that even the basic staples of life, such as meat, eggs, flour, and sugar, were exported, leaving the average citizen with nothing. Although Romania had the potential to be a rich nation agriculturally, and already was in some respects, it was now starving due to state policy.

Ceausescu was so intent on saving national resources for export by any means possible, that he made a decree for all bakeries in the country to sell only day-old bread. This meant that once bread was freshly baked, it must be stored for at least one day before it was made available to the public. Ceausescu's rationale for this was that day-old bread did not taste as good as bread freshly baked; therefore, the populous would consume less. That, in turn, meant that more flour and wheat would be available to export to Western Europe. Romania even produced two types of chocolate: one for export (with cocoa beans) and one for Romanians (without). Imagine chocolate without any cocoa! A Romanian friend whose sister worked at the chocolate export factory said that armed guards would stand behind production line employees to ensure none of the quality chocolate was stolen. It was this disregard for the welfare of his own citizens that made Ceausescu so hated.

Born in 1918 into poverty as one of nine children in a small Romanian village, young Nicolae Ceausescu took quickly to the budding philosophy of communism. As a member of the communist youth movement, Nicolae was frequently in and out of trouble with governmental authorities. When the communist party's power and prestige began to grow in Romania, Ceausescu advanced in its ranks of leadership. At the age of twenty-one, he met Elena Petrescu. Elena was also from a peasant family with only an elementary school education, and eventually, she would become his dictatorial partner in life. The two were married in 1947. Nicolae took over the reins of the Romanian Communist Party as General Secretary almost two decades later in 1965, not to be dethroned from power until his and Elena's violent deaths on Christmas day, 1989.

Their tyrannical decades of rule over Romania propelled the nation into becoming one of Europe's poorest countries. Living a life of opulence while their country starved, both Nicolae and Elena could not care less about the suffering of their nation's citizens. In his later years, Nicolae was known for his extreme paranoia, living in constant fear that he would one day be assassinated. A germaphobe, he rarely wore the same suit twice. He spent his evenings in the private movie theater that he had built for himself watching the 1970s American crime drama, "Kojak," starring the late Telly Savalas.

Elena spent her time spying on other members of the communist party leadership. She had the Securitate, the Romanian Secret Police, plant hidden cameras and microphones in their homes and offices. Elena especially enjoyed secretly recording the bedroom activities of her comrades and used many a recording as political leverage against her enemies. Insecure to her core, Elena made sure that wherever she went internationally, she was offered an honorary doctorate degree in some field of science, despite only having a grammar school pedigree. Elena required those in her orbit to refer to her as the Chief Scientist of Romania.

It was because of the severe repression of an entire nation by these two tyrants that I was now engaged in Bible smuggling. Karl Marx, one of communism's luminaries, had once called religion the opiate of the masses. Both Nicolae and Elena Ceausescu, throughout their years in power, did their best to crush all forms of Christianity under the foot of Romanian communism.

Rows of trees with white-painted tree trunks lined both sides of the two-lane road as we drew closer to Arad. On either side of us were open fields that were dotted with an occasional farm that was in a sorry state of repair.

A brief stop at a roadway turnout allowed us to consolidate all of the articles intended for the evangelism project. The items were placed into large bags that also held gifts for our contacts. This would allow us to make a quick and inconspicuous exit from the Nissan once we parked in the city's downtown district.

We talked casually as the city limits drew closer, which was apparent by the decrease of countryside and the increase of concrete bloc tenement buildings. What would the communists ever have done without the invention of concrete? Row after row of these hideous, unfinished structures made up the landscape of every major city in Romania. Not only were they aesthetically distasteful, but the sub-standard construction made them dangerous as well. The majority of city dwellers lived in such glorified shelters and had, on average, small, two-room apartments.

The first object of interest to us as we entered Arad was the incredible line for gas at the nationally owned Peco gas station. People would often queue for up to two days, many parking their cars in line overnight as they awaited their turn at the pumps. In a picture of contrast, Westerners who would purchase coupons for fuel at the border were not required to wait in these long gas lines. In an attempt to encourage tourism, the Romanian government didn't want those paying with hard currency to experience the same inconveniences as the rest of Romania's citizens. It was always an uncomfortable feeling zipping to the head of those gas lines and looking into the dejected and often angry faces of people whose suffering I could only imagine.

Once inside such a large, urbanized area, the eyes of the populous tended to focus their attention on our vehicle. Fortunately, our Nissan somewhat resembled the Romanian built four-wheel drive Aero. But on closer inspection by even the average citizen standing in a bread line or walking down the sidewalk, it was obvious that we were not Romanian.

After numerous smuggling trips and countless briefings with fellow Bible smugglers, I had a standardized plan of action upon entering a city. This plan would vary somewhat from trip to trip in order to avoid detection. We parked our vehicle in a part of town where it would not appear out of place. Such locations often included hotel or restaurant parking lots, as well as parking areas often frequented by tourists in a central part of downtown. Where we parked the Nissan depended on where it had been parked the last time it had visited Arad.

Our choice this day was a busy side street not too far from the central downtown shopping areas. From this point, until we were safely inside our contact's home, we would not be able to talk unless it was absolutely necessary. Daylight visitations were very dangerous, not only for us but also for those with whom we were visiting.

We exited the Nissan taking the bags of goodies with us as we secured all the doors. A quick prayer of protection for the car and its remaining contents was all that could be done now to ensure its safety. Even the so-called utopian Communist state of Romania had its share of crime, and a loaded Western vehicle was a prime target.

Don followed me quietly down the sidewalk since I was the one who knew where we were going. It was hard to appear to be nonchalantly going on a walk when we were carrying such heavy bags. Good walking shoes were a must since a hike of several miles was not uncommon. On this day, with many kilometers still to travel, we had parked somewhat closer to our contact's home. For that, my sore shoulders and back were extremely grateful.

We approached T.T.'s home (our contact's nickname), and I made one final visual sweep of the area to ensure that we were not being watched. We rang the electric bell on the large steel gate and waited for someone to arrive. In a matter of seconds, T.T.'s wife appeared. She immediately recognized me and opened the gate, allowing us to enter the home's large courtyard.

We were quickly ushered inside and immediately welcomed with smiles, hugs, and open arms. T.T., an architect by profession, had a passion for evangelism. Since creative architectural design was not a priority for Romania's communist government, he tapped his creative energies and directed them toward spreading God's Word under difficult circumstances. His new evangelism outreach into Romanian orphanages was a good example.

T.T. was very excited that we had arrived safely with our shipment of novelties. His co-workers could now begin the task of assembling the items into individual packets for distribution at Easter. On a subsequent visit, I was informed that the outreach had been an amazing success. The impact these packets had on the lives of otherwise forgotten Romanian orphans was staggering. Not only were the orphans themselves touched, but those working at the orphanage found it hard to believe that Christians would go to such lengths to share God's love with those under their care. T.T.'s team of evangelists were able to share Jesus Christ with the entire orphanage.

We enjoyed about an hour of fellowship with T.T. and his family, and soon it was time to be on our way again. Saying goodbye was always difficult since the nature of our work together made future contact uncertain. It was not uncommon to receive information through our secret telephone network that a contact had been compromised, meaning no future meetings could take place. T.T. was about to undertake a highly visible evangelism project, and the potential for this eventuality could not be ruled out.

We said our final goodbyes and made our last embraces, and Don and I slipped out the front gate as quietly and as quickly as we had entered. Our walk back to the Nissan was made easier by the now-empty bags that hung from our shoulders. A few minutes later, we were safely inside the Nissan and starting the engine for the last major portion of the day's journey.

It was now late afternoon. Darkness would be necessary for the next phase of our adventure. However, we had to make it to Oradea first. We drove down the city streets of Arad and made our way to the outskirts of town and the small, two-lane road that would lead us north. Our conversation began to focus on the events ahead.

The bustle of city traffic now yielded to an occasional car or horse-drawn cart that shared our stretch of roadway. We passed through village after village as we plodded along at what would be an unusually slow pace for Western highways. Each town we passed resembled the last, with nothing but a sign with its name to distinguish it from the others along our way. Even the communist party billboards praising Ceausescu began to get monotonous.

Don and I now discussed our action plan in regard to what would take place over the next several hours. Entering the most dangerous phase of our mission, it was critical that there could be no misunderstandings. Mistakes would not only endanger us, our vehicle, and our mission, but they had the potential to expose our Romanian contacts to extreme danger as well. If we were discovered, the consequences would be unpleasant, to say the least. For us, after several days of interrogation and the confiscation of our vehicle, we would eventually be allowed to leave Romania. Our contacts, of course, would not have it so easy. The fear of potential repercussions for our contacts kept me not only on my toes but on my knees as well. These men and women were part of my family now, and they had families of their own that they were putting at risk to follow God's call on their lives. With the help of the Lord, I was determined that I would not be the one to compromise their ministry and endanger their loved ones.

We arrived safely in Oradea at dusk. With the exception of the tension that filled the Nissan's cab due to what we were about to undertake, our trip had been uneventful. The Nissan Patrol had always mechanically been a dependable vehicle. One breakdown or flat tire in Eastern Europe would have added unimaginable complications to a mission. Our safe arrival after traversing countless hours of Eastern European roads in both Hungary and Romania was a blessing not to be overlooked.

Don and I parked in a part of the city that would allow us to sit unnoticed until nightfall. We would wait until absolute darkness before proceeding to the address of our contact. This was a time for quiet reflection and prayer. Any joking or lighthearted conversation had stopped long ago. What was ahead was deadly serious business.

With our mission now covered by prayer and a cloak of darkness, we started the engine and made our way to the northwestern portion of the city. This was familiar territory to me. We would drive directly to a location that I had determined would be secure for us to leave the vehicle for a few hours.

We were now several blocks away from our contact's home in one of Romania's typical apartment complexes. I eased the Patrol into a parking space in an unlit portion of a large hospital parking lot with several trucks parked in our vicinity; the Nissan's presence was fairly well disguised.

Tonight, Don would follow me at a much further distance. I would meet him just inside the building's main door, which was out of sight for anyone who might be traveling on the sidewalk or street. We were both once again loaded with gifts for our contact, John, and his family. His son loved bananas, so I had done my best to bring some with me. The cold weather had again turned what had been yellow bananas, unfortunately black. But they would still be a treasure to a Romanian.

I exited the Patrol first and made my way across the street to the sidewalk that ran in front of John's apartment. Moving slowly, head down so as not to make eye contact with anyone or attract undue attention, I started down the street. A minute later, Don would repeat my steps.

As I approached the building, I was happy to see that it was experiencing an all-too-common power blackout. Although this would make it a little more difficult for Don to see the building number, it would help us avoid visible contact with strangers. I entered the building foyer and found it to be empty. I waited inside the door with my eyes glued to the sidewalk. In case Don missed the building and continued down the sidewalk, I needed to be able to intercept him. However, right on schedule, Don turned from the sidewalk toward the building as if he had visited this location a thousand times.

Without a word exchanged between us, we made our way up the flight of stairs. With no lights in the building, the stairwell was extremely dark. Memory directed me to John's apartment on the third floor, and our quiet knock was answered almost immediately.

The next few minutes were filled with introductions, hugs, and kisses on the cheek, which are common in Eastern Europe. Everyone was happy to see me again, they were glad to meet Don, and they were ecstatic over the gifts of food and candy we had brought for the children.

We enjoyed a wonderful meal and after the normal update on each of our families, we began to settle into our business discussions. John gave us a brief update on the situation in Romania, indicating in a nutshell that things had only continued to worsen.

John and I began to discuss logistical problems with our literature pipeline to Romanian Moldavia. Moldavia, in northeastern Romania, had seen very little Christian literature since the rise of communism. Oradea, on the other hand, being a western border city, continued to receive a disproportionate amount of literature. It was easier for Western mission agencies to drop their loads of Scripture immediately inside Romania; therefore, much of the smuggled literature arriving never left the western portion of the country.

Due to this problem, John and I had been trying to develop a smuggling pipeline to the northeastern part of Romania. This was proving to be difficult. If I were to travel to Moldavia with a Western vehicle, it would be very dangerous. Westerners in this region of the country were extremely rare, making the Nissan stand out like a sore thumb and almost guaranteeing complications for any smuggling endeavor. Additionally, every major city in Romania had police checkpoints on all key roads leading out of their city limits. Travelers were also often subjected to surprise checkpoints throughout Romania's road system. This made travel with large amounts of literature extremely dangerous, especially for Romanian citizens who would have no means to hide their contraband.

Though we had achieved only limited success in getting small quantities of literature up north, John and I agreed that we would intensify our efforts. Our goal was more literature saturation for Moldavia. Just as the children of Israel had been ordered to possess the land of Canaan, we were not about to be defeated in our efforts to spread the Gospel of Christ throughout Romania.

Our discussion now shifted to this evening's events. John was having difficulty locating what he considered to be a secure location for the unloading of the vehicle's "system." The process took, on average, thirty to forty minutes of uninterrupted work, and it required absolute privacy. Not only was the work tedious, but it was also nerve-racking. If one did not have the proper amount of time and the right surroundings, catastrophic mistakes could result.

John informed us that he had made arrangements for us to travel to a village just outside of Oradea to unload the Patrol. The house where we would do the work had a large, enclosed courtyard to ensure privacy, and it was owned by a trustworthy member of John's church. An all-village event was taking place in the community that evening, ensuring that most nosy neighbors would not be at home. With no viable alternative, I agreed, and we began to prepare to leave as John made a quick telephone call to set the evening's events into motion.

The plan was to follow John in his car to the outskirts of the city and then leave his vehicle in a parking lot. From there, we would travel together to the village that was less than ten kilometers further. I was somewhat uncomfortable with this proposal, due in part to a Romanian law that did not allow Romanians to travel with foreigners if the trip had not been approved by the government. I was afraid of the possibility of being stopped by the police with John in the car. I had nightmares of this nature. John assured me that the road we would be using had no police checkpoints, and because we were traveling such a short distance, the chances of being stopped were minimal.

Reluctantly I agreed, and we said our final goodbyes to John's family. I retraced my steps back to the Nissan, and a minute later, I was joined by Don.

We started the Patrol and pulled out onto the road in front of John's house, doubling back behind his apartment building to an alley where John's car was waiting. Noticing the Patrol behind him, John immediately started his engine and turned right onto the road that ran parallel to his apartment. I followed, not too closely, but close enough not to lose him in the dark nighttime traffic. Almost all Romanian cars looked alike!

We made our way through town, arriving at the destination where John was to leave his car. With no one in sight, John jumped into the passenger seat with Don riding in back. John directed me to the road we would take that led out of town. Less than a minute later, we had left the city limits of Oradea and were headed into the countryside.

Just as John had predicted, there were no police checkpoints along our way. We arrived in the village, and it looked deserted. We made our way down several side streets, and I noticed that there wasn't a single person outdoors. This was unusual in Romania, where villagers left for their factory jobs at all hours of the day and night.

Just like an old James Bond movie, the gate to the compound of the home swung open once we entered the driveway. I drove into the courtyard, and the gate was closed behind us by a man who was obviously expecting guests. I pulled the Patrol to a stop just under what appeared to be a lit carport, and we were instantly greeted with hugs and kisses by three fellow believers.

The location John had chosen for unloading the Patrol was perfect. The home was located inside an enclosed compound with a backyard, high walls, and plenty of foliage to ensure privacy. There was a short time for introductions, and then I went straight to work unloading the system, requesting privacy from our new friends.

I began to work methodically, like a robot who had performed the same function countless times before. Initial entry into the system was difficult and required precision. One wrong move at this stage could accidentally damage the compartment's closing mechanism, meaning the entire compartment would not be able to be closed for the trip home. That was a frightening prospect considering the fact that border inspections leaving the country were just as tight as entering.

Once past the first stage of the operation, the task remaining was not as difficult as it was time-consuming. I progressed toward entry into the main compartment and noticed that everyone in the courtyard had gravitated to within feet of the vehicle with their curiosity piqued. At this point, exhausted from the pressures of the last two days, I was not about to make an issue of the fact that these men were now watching something that was extremely secret. I reasoned to myself that I was dead anyway if one of these guys decided to talk about what they already knew, so a little more knowledge on their part wouldn't change my circumstances. I did ask John to tell the men that what they were witnessing was to remain confidential, for whatever that was worth.

It was fun to see the expressions on their faces as I progressed toward opening the literature compartment. It was obvious that they were impressed with the technology and ingenuity that went into the design of our smuggling vehicle. I opened the final latch that allowed me to open the hatch of the literature compartment, and all eyes were transfixed on what they were witnessing.

As the literature compartment opened to reveal a host of New Testaments and Christian literature, one of the three men could not contain his excitement. He jumped up and down, screaming and yelling and praising the Lord. It took several seconds for the other men to calm him enough for him to realize he was jeopardizing our entire operation with his rejoicing!

The Patrol's contents were quickly unloaded and taken inside the house. I now began the process of closing the compartment, which meant going through exactly the opposite process of what I had just done.

After a few minutes, there was no evidence that the Nissan was any different from the score of other Patrols that had at one time rolled off a Japanese assembly line. I finished my job and walked into the house, where I found all the brothers admiring the literature that was spread out on a long table.

We had a brief discussion about the literature and then gathered around to thank the Lord for His protection and to commit the smuggled Scripture into God's further care. What lay spread out before us was the result of countless miracles that had been orchestrated by our Father. We knew that we had side-stepped many perils with the Lord's help to get to this point. My prayer was one of thanksgiving.

We concluded our prayer time together, and John informed me that the bulk of the literature would be hidden at that home until it could be moved safely in small quantities to other safe havens. It would then hopefully enter our distribution pipeline north.

John began packing a suitcase of literature that he said was needed immediately in Oradea. The plan was that John, along with another man from his group, would be dropped off in Oradea to safely store the literature. Don and I would then continue to our hotel to check-in for the evening.

I immediately felt uncomfortable with this scenario. We would not only now be traveling with two Romanians in our vehicle, but also a clearly visible suitcase of literature. If we were stopped by the police, trouble would be guaranteed. I expressed my concerns to John, who, in turn, reminded me of the ease by which we had arrived in the village. No checkpoint, remember? John had a way of making everything sound so easy. It was true that we had not had any problems on our way from Oradea to this village, and I did have a tendency to be over-cautious. Maybe I was overreacting to the potential for danger in this short ten-minute drive. With misgivings, but fairly convinced that we had nothing to fear, I agreed to take the literature and the men back to Oradea.

We said our goodbyes as the brothers continued to thank us profusely for what we had just delivered to their nation. We jumped in the Nissan with John in front to make sure that I didn't make any wrong turns along the way. Don and the other man were in the backseat. Once again, our host quietly opened the gate. I eased the Nissan through the opening and pulled onto the dirt road with our lights off to avoid unwanted attention.

Once safely several hundred yards from the house, I turned the lights back on for our final journey of the evening. The Patrol's diesel motor was uncomfortably loud to me as we drove past the darkened homes of the villagers. Unfortunately, noisy diesel engines were a necessity in Eastern Europe as other forms of fuel were scarce.

We turned from the small dirt road that led out of the village onto the paved, two-lane road that led into Oradea. We talked quietly among ourselves about the events of the evening. All of us were excited about how successful the night had been and how the Lord had protected our every move.

As we rounded a bend in the road, my heart stopped with terror at what I saw before us. One hundred yards in front of the Nissan, I recognized what could only be the reflective baton of a police officer who was standing in the middle of the road.

John, who noticed it as well, was frozen in silence. In a matter of seconds, we would reach the policeman. There was no time for thinking, praying, or anything else. Our fate was totally in God's hands.

The reflective baton, which had been held at the side of whoever was in front of us, now began to wave slowly over his head, indicating that we were to pull over. As I turned around to Don and the man in the back seat, the concern on their faces was painfully obvious.

"No talking," I said to both of them as I turned to look at John in the passenger seat next to me. "You only speak

English," I directed. He was clearly shaken by what was about to take place. He looked directly at me, and with a heavy Romanian accent, said, "I only speak English." Looking at his facial characteristics, which were so typically Romanian, and hearing his accent, I wasn't very reassured.

The officer was clearly visible now. I slowed our speed to a crawl as I pulled to the right shoulder of the road. I came to a complete stop once the officer's location in the middle of the roadway was directly parallel to my driver's side window.

He approached the Nissan, and I noticed a flashlight in his other hand. These guys never have flashlights, and when they do, they never have the batteries to operate them! I rolled down my window. Being led by the Holy Spirit, I pulled my passport out of my pocket and leaned forward, obstructing the view of the passenger seat.

"Americans," I said to the officer. On came the flashlight as the officer shone it in my face and then down onto my passport. After what seemed an eternity, he moved to the front of the car and shined the flashlight into the front windshield, examining the passengers and contents of our vehicle.

My heart was beating so fast I was sure the officer outside could hear it. Time stood still. I was so stunned by these events that I could not even think. The only thing any of us could do now was to sit and wait for whatever would happen next.

Once again, God's miraculous intervention was made manifest in our hour of need. Turning off his flashlight, the policeman again moved to my driver's side window. With a final penetrating gaze, as if he knew everything we were up to, the officer waved his baton to indicate that we could proceed. During the entire encounter, he never spoke a word!

We began to roll now, putting distance between ourselves and the checkpoint. The Nissan was filled with a chorus of praises to the King of Kings, that is, after we were able to breathe again. Just like Joshua and Caleb returning from Canaan, we would be returning to Germany with a good report.

CHAPTER FOUR
POSSESS THE LAND

By the summer of 1989, after almost a year of traveling
in Eastern Europe, I was now becoming a seasoned Bible
smuggler. That being said, I had yet to travel to Bulgaria
on assignment. I was particularly concerned about my
first scheduled trip there, due in part to Bulgaria's use of
the Cyrillic alphabet that resembled hieroglyphics to me.
Navigating in Bulgaria while trying not to draw attention
to myself when I could not read signs, ask for directions, or
seek assistance posed a problem. Little did I know that my
concerns were warranted.

The director of our Finnish office, Ignat (Ivo) Ivanov, was
an ethnic Bulgarian who had married a Finnish national.
Ivo's extended family, who lived in Bulgaria, were Mission
Possible's pipeline into the country, with both of his brothers
serving as pastors in the capital city of Sofia. The plan for
me was to again use the Nissan Patrol, which had seldom
traveled into Bulgaria, as my covert mode of transportation.
In the secret compartment, I would be smuggling a shipment
of Bibles and New Testaments in the Bulgarian language,
bound for believers in Sofia. Pavel, Ivo's eldest brother,
would be my point of contact.

Since the common use of email for the average person was a thing of the future, telephone calls, with coded messages in the conversations, would be the primary way I would establish my travel itinerary with Pavel. As Pavel's English was limited, and my Bulgarian was non-existent, Ivo and his wife, Mirjami, would be the ones contacting Pavel for me. Through these coded messages, a time and date were set for me to arrive at Pavel's house on the outskirts of Sofia. I now needed from Ivo and Mirjami detailed navigation instructions to Pavel's home. I would not have the assistance of modern GPS technology, nor street signs that I could read easily. Mirjami, whose English was much better than Ivo's, would be my tutor in finding my way in Bulgaria.

As with similar trips to Romania, my plan for this journey to Bulgaria was to pose as a tour guide, albeit this time for a country I had yet to visit. My traveling companion would be a young man about my age, James, from a mission organization based in Vienna, Austria. Since Vienna was not far out of the way, I would travel to Austria, pick James up, and then continue to Bulgaria – reversing the trip upon our return. James was a new acquaintance to me. He had never been to Bulgaria, nor had he ever been on a Bible smuggling operation. While I was confident in the travel skills I had acquired in the previous year, I was hoping that James would bring to the table some yet undetermined talent of his own that would aid our journey.

Through Mirjami, our trip was scheduled for a month in the future. As my departure date approached, our well-crafted travel plans began to go south. For random reasons, the date of our trip had to be changed numerous times. This was due to problems in Bulgaria and at our German office. Mirjami did her best to coordinate these changes with Pavel, but after our plans had been altered so often, the rudimentary code words we used for communication could no longer keep up with the constantly changing itinerary. Just prior to my departure, Mirjami called to inform me that she was unsure if Pavel was clear in regard to our exact arrival date and time. At this point, there should have been no question that I heed the warning sirens going off in my head, but the trip continued as planned. Mirjami assured me that she would continue her attempts to communicate with Pavel to make him aware of our itinerary.

The Nissan was packed in preparation, and on the appointed Wednesday morning of my departure, I set off toward Vienna. Suzi, the young neighbor girl from across the street, had invited me to have coffee with her family the following Sunday. I agreed, as I knew that I would be home from Bulgaria on Saturday evening at the latest.

The drive through the Austrian Alps skirting the city of Salzburg was always beautiful, and this summer day was no exception. I was in good spirits, and everything was going to plan. I pulled into Baden, a suburb of Vienna, mid-morning as scheduled. James was packed and ready to go. Our goal was to travel a few more hours to the Yugoslavian border, and then make a long push to Belgrade, Serbia, before bedding down for the night. We would then continue the next day for the much shorter trip to Sofia.

Prior to the breakup of the Eastern Block, Yugoslavia was comprised of six republics: Bosnia and Herzegovina, Croatia, Macedonia, Montenegro, Serbia, and Slovenia. Our trip was to take us through Slovenia and then continue through the republics of Croatia and Serbia. This would be my first trip to visit any of these republics.

As was my custom, I spent the majority of our first few hours of travel briefing James on what to expect and how to act during our upcoming border crossings. The distance between Vienna and Slovenia gave us ample time to cover all of the information necessary to prepare James for what might lie ahead. That being said, no level of preparedness can ease the nervous feeling one gets when approaching a communist border crossing with a vehicle full of hidden Bibles.

Fortunately for us, our crossing into Yugoslavia went off without a hitch. The tight controls at this border had been significantly eased over the past few years, as had been the case in Hungary, and we were reaping the benefits of the new "openness" that was beginning to spread across Eastern Europe. The long drive across Croatia and into Serbia lay before us. Although some multi-lane highways existed, much of our drive would be on two-lane roads. We pulled into Belgrade late Wednesday evening, exhausted from the long day of travel.

Our drive the next day, Thursday, which was our appointed date to arrive in Sofia, would not be so arduous. An early morning departure from Belgrade would allow us to arrive late morning if we had no problems on the road or at the Bulgarian frontier. It was another beautiful day for travel. The journey through Serbia into Bulgaria went without any problems and was amazingly pleasant. Few cars were lined up when we arrived at the Bulgarian border, and to my surprise, our entry into the country took place without a physical inspection of our vehicle. We were across the frontier in less than ten minutes! This trip was shaping up to be a walk in the park!

My euphoria on having easily completed two successful border crossings in the last two days was short-lived as I now began to notice almost every sign on the road ahead of me was written in Cyrillic script. Unfortunately, while I still had not figured out James' undetermined talent, mastery of the Cyrillic alphabet was not it.

We managed to make good time from the Bulgarian border to the outskirts of Sofia. All was going well, and if Mirjami's communication of our arrival date and time with Pavel had worked, he would be expecting us early afternoon. My plan was to drive into Sofia and check into our hotel, and then leave James to explore the downtown area while I took the Nissan to meet Pavel. Since James had no knowledge of where I was going or with whom I was meeting, I surmised that having him accompany me would only be a complication – especially if we were to get caught. He was much more likely to stay out of trouble roaming the streets of Sofia as a tourist.

One of the few Western hotels in Sofia in 1989 was the downtown Sheraton. Foreigners were required to stay in particular hotels in the city, so I was extremely happy that the Sheraton was one of my only options. Few perks came with Bible smuggling, but I counted two nights of luxurious hotel living among them. James and I checked into our rooms and then went down to the hotel restaurant for a quick lunch. I had approximately an hour before I needed to be on my way to Pavel.

As James and I finished lunch, I coached him on what his afternoon activities should look like in my absence so as not to draw too much attention to himself. We said our goodbyes, and I pulled the Patrol out of the Sheraton's parking lot and onto the capital's busy streets. I made my way toward the outskirts of town. Leaving the bustle of the metropolitan area for the residential fringes of Sofia, I was now relying on my memory of conversations with Mirjami to find my way. The Bulgarian street signs were of no use. From the appearance of things, it looked like I might be entering the correct section of town; however, with no real frame of reference other than a telephone conversation, it was hard to tell.

I was now becoming confused. Everything looked the same. I found myself in block after block of residential housing, none of it unique. Every street block and every house looked just like the next. It did not help matters that street signs were now scarce. Even though I could not read the Cyrillic alphabet, letters of an address could be matched with a lucky street sign – if only there was a street sign. I began to panic.

Since driving around in circles looking for the appropriate street name and house number would draw far too much attention to my Western vehicle, I pulled the Nissan off to the side of the street in this residential neighborhood and began to frantically pray. I was truly at the end of my rope. While I did have a street address and house number, I had nothing else. I was not given Pavel's telephone number since we would not have been able to communicate because of our language barrier.

I prayed and decided that I should circle the block on foot. Maybe by doing this, I would find a street name on a sign or locate a house with a street name and house number attached to it – anything. I had to do something. Since I had to leave the car unattended while it was fully loaded with literature, I parked it out of the way so that it would not be noticeable to those in the neighborhood. I locked the doors of the Patrol and set out on foot.

I made my way down the first street of the block of houses I was planning to circle and silently began to pray once again. In a few moments, I knew that this jaunt was not helping. No signs. No street names. Even if the house did not have a gate, fence, or wall that obscured the house number, there was still no way of determining if I was close to being on the correct street. I walked as slowly as I dared in order not to draw attention, but I soon found myself back where I had started – at the Nissan.

I decided that I could safely make one final loop around the neighboring block of houses before my wandering of the neighborhood would draw too much attention and alert a nosy resident to call the police. Everything to this point had gone so well. What would I do if I had to abort the mission and figure out a new plan for the contents of my vehicle? With one final prayer of desperation, asking the Lord to make a way in this impossible situation, I started once again to walk the neighboring block of houses.

I moved down the first street of the new block just as slowly as I dared...nothing. This was my last chance to find Pavel before the mission had to be aborted. I unhurriedly approached the midway point of the street, and a door swung open on a house to my right. I looked closely, and I couldn't believe my eyes. It was Pavel! He called to me in Bulgarian and motioned for me to come inside his home. God had done it – He had made a way in the midst of my utter helplessness.

Things now began to happen quickly. I was unable to converse with Pavel, so we improvised until we could get help with translation. After a few minutes, the Nissan was retrieved, and the literature was safely off-loaded at the back of Pavel's house away from prying and curious eyes. Once the unpacking was complete, we continued to wait patiently together in Pavel's home for the translator. The entire time, I was giving praise and glory to God. Little did I realize the rest of the story that was about to be revealed.

Once someone arrived to help us with our communication, Pavel explained to me the magnitude of the miracle that had just transpired. He began by explaining the confusion that had taken place as a result of his numerous telephone conversations with Mirjami. Initially, he had understood when I was planning to arrive, but as call after call continued to take place, my arrival date became a jumbled mess – to the point that Pavel had no idea what date or time I would be coming to Bulgaria. My arrival had been a total unknown.

Fast forward to the events of the day. Pavel had been planning to go to work at the church in Sofia like he did every morning, but today, God specifically told him to remain home. Pavel had no idea why. We would both find out later that Mirjami had continued for days to try to call Pavel in order to clarify our arrival time, but the international phone lines had been down since I had departed Germany. She had not been able to complete her call.

While Pavel busied himself around the house, not knowing why he was staying home from work, he received a phone call. It was from Mirjami in Finland who was able to finally connect, letting him know that I would be arriving that day. Pavel received the call at the exact moment that I turned down his street. Additionally, Pavel's phone was located away from the main body of his house in a small annex, or winter garden area. The phone sat on a table underneath a small window that had a direct view of the street – in the direction I was walking. The telephone rang, and Pavel answered the call from Finland that told him I was arriving. He then simultaneously looked out the window and saw me approaching, just as I gasped my last prayer for help.

In comparison to the events that had surrounded my arrival in Sofia, Friday's activities were tame. We did get the chance to meet and fellowship with some of the members of Pavel's congregation, and that was a treat. For a Bible smuggler, contact with larger groups of believers in most of Eastern Europe was usually frowned upon, due in part to the danger it posed for the national believers.

James and I said farewell to the Bulgarian team and prepared to depart Sofia from our luxurious accommodations at the Sheraton early on the third morning of our visit. We planned to leave Saturday and drive all the way through to Vienna. James had a business appointment on Sunday, and I had a coffee date with my neighbors Sunday afternoon.

Very early on Saturday, our final day in Bulgaria, James and I loaded up our few belongings and pointed the Nissan westward toward home. We were excited as we thought about what had just been accomplished with the Lord's help. We had been a part of another successful smuggling mission.

While frontier crossings leaving Eastern Europe were usually less stressful than the ones entering (primarily because we were traveling with an empty secret compartment in our vehicle), they were not without cause for worry. I had once spent hours leaving the Hungarian border as they took apart my van piece by piece. Fortunately, on that trip, I had been traveling with a normal vehicle that had not been designed for smuggling, and the Hungarian border guards had found nothing. So, as we approached the Bulgarian border with Yugoslavia, we were cautiously optimistic that we had no reason to worry. We were correct, as our border crossing back into Serbia took only a matter of minutes.

James and I made good time as we zipped across Serbia, passing through Belgrade again on our way to Croatia. As we closed in on the Serbian/Croatian border, the roads began to deteriorate. We had traveled on major highways through much of Serbia, but now as we approached Croatia, we had to slow our pace because of the much smaller and more congested two-lane roads. James and I passed the time chatting about the events of the past few days. Because there were no internal border crossings within Yugoslavia, it was hard to know where Serbia ended and Croatia began.

Suddenly, as we entered the outskirts of the eastern Croatian city of Slavonski Brod, we noticed a police officer on the side of the road waving a baton directing me to pull over. I was confused as to why I was being flagged down. The area where I was being stopped was quite rural, and the city of Slavonski Brod was still several miles ahead of us. I was always careful with my driving while in Eastern Europe, and as far as I knew, I had been going the speed limit due in part to the heavy traffic on this two-lane highway.

As we approached the police officer, I noticed that he had "set up shop" in an area that afforded the possibility of several cars being pulled over at the same time. Our vehicle was not the only Western car that had been stopped. The officer did not approach the Nissan, so after waiting what I deemed was an excessive period of time, I exited the Patrol and walked over to him.

In broken English, the officer demanded my passport and said, "Speeding. Radar." Radar was not yet commonplace, especially in Eastern Europe, so I was immediately suspect. The policeman added, "You broke the law and passed three cars." Now I knew I was being railroaded. I hadn't passed a car for miles due to the heavy traffic we had been following on this congested strip of roadway.

It was at this point that I made the day's first mistake. I should have immediately realized that a single Andrew Jackson placed in this officer's hands would have sent me back on my merry way. However, not recognizing what was really happening, I became defensive and immediately tried to argue my case with a man who didn't speak English.

Two things happened next. First, my protests of innocence, which the officer obviously could not understand, were making him angrier by the second. Second, as it became evident to him that the Andrew Jackson would not be making an appearance, he slapped me across the left side of my head hard enough to make me stagger backward.

The officer turned red with rage as he yelled, "GO!"

I was in a state of shock. I had just been physically assaulted, and the man who had done it was still holding my passport.

"But you have my passport," I protested.

"GO!" the officer yelled again.

I could tell that a second physical altercation was about to take place if I did not heed his instructions. I turned around in total bewilderment and got back into the Nissan. Before I pulled away, the officer shoved a piece of paper, a receipt of some kind, in my direction, and motioned to me to get moving. I drove off.

What had just happened? I began to process with James the events of the last few minutes, and panic began to come over me. I no longer had my passport. How was I supposed to get it back? I had no idea. The only thing I knew was that this police officer had not been rational, and there was no going back to him to retrieve my passport.

By this time, it was mid-afternoon on Saturday. In the recesses of my mind, a plan began to formulate, and I discussed my new strategy with James. Zagreb, the capital of Croatia, was only a few hours ahead of us. My idea was that we would pull into Zagreb, spend the weekend, and visit the US consulate on Monday. We could then explain the circumstances of the day's events and ask for their intervention. Good plan.

It was at this point that James reminded me that he had to be back in Vienna that evening for meetings the next day. When I asked James if it might be possible for him to miss these meetings due to these new, unforeseen circumstances, he became adamant that he had to get back to Vienna on time. I was still looking for James' undetermined talent, and it certainly was not compassion for others in need.

In light of this new revelation, I altered my plan a bit. I would drive James past Zagreb all the way to the Yugoslav/Austrian border and let him out. He would have to cross on his own, on foot, and then either have to find a bus, train, or hitchhike his way back to Vienna. I would turn around and head back to Zagreb. It was going to be a long evening of driving, but it would work.

We were still several hours from the border, and the mood in the vehicle had unquestionably soured. James was not too happy with my plan to abandon him at the border. I also think he was a bit miffed at the circumstances that had just transpired between myself and the police officer, forcing him to complete the journey by himself.

It was twilight by the time we reached the Yugoslav/ Austrian border. A long line of cars was in front of us, snaking their way to the first checkpoint on the Yugoslavian side of the frontier. As I impatiently waited to get James a little closer to the border before letting him out, the genesis of the day's second mistake began to formulate in my mind. I could now clearly see the Yugoslavian border crossing. Because of the long line, Yugoslavian border guards were allowing many cars to pass through without checking any passport documentation whatsoever. In fact, most cars were approaching the Austrian side of the border unchecked. It appeared that the Yugoslavian border police were only randomly asking for passports.

What if I was able to cross the Yugoslavian side of the border without having to show my passport? If I could do this, then I was sure that once I arrived at the Austrian checkpoint, everything would be fine. I could enter their office, explain to them the circumstances of why I no longer was in possession of my passport, show them my German driver's license to prove my German residency, and request passage to Vienna where I could get a new passport from the US embassy in Vienna. The Austrians were reasonable people. This plan now seemed infinitely better than my previous idea that would, at some point, require me to engage with the authorities who had physically assaulted me. I didn't have long to make my decision, so as we inched closer to the guardhouse, I informed James of my new strategy.

And, to my amazement, we were waved right through. To say that I was thrilled is an understatement. While I had hoped that the plan would work, I had estimated my chances were fifty-fifty at best. It had gone perfectly, and now we were moving closer to wonderful Austria. No more inflexible Eastern Europeans. I would now deal with rational Westerners like myself. No problem.

We pulled up to the Austrian checkpoint, and I rolled down my window and informed the border police officer of my predicament. His response was less than encouraging. In fact, it was quite troubling. With a look of disgust on his face, he told me to park the Nissan and go inside and explain my dilemma to his superiors. Once inside, things did not go any better. There really wasn't even a debate. Under absolutely no circumstance would I be allowed to enter Austria without a passport. I was told to turn the car around and go back to Yugoslavia, end of discussion.

If I thought that I had been in trouble earlier, I was redefining the word at this point. Horror came over me as I realized that I was now going to have to turn around and try to re-enter Yugoslavia without a passport! I was in the middle of no man's land!

By this point, James was done with me. With his passport in hand, he was now free to go on his way. He took his small bag out of the Patrol, we said our goodbyes, and he disappeared on foot into the darkness of traffic moving toward the West. While I had never discovered any undetermined talent for James, the adage, "two heads are better than one," came to mind as I watched him walk into the night. I turned the car around and headed back toward Yugoslavia like a dog with his tail tucked between his legs.

I can't remember in my many travels having to beg to be allowed to enter a country I had no desire to visit, but on this day, I begged! The evening was now getting late, and I beseeched and pleaded with customs officials to let me into Yugoslavia without a passport. In the end, the slip of paper given to me by the police officer was my saving grace. Apparently, although I couldn't read it, it was a receipt confirming the confiscation of my passport. This proved enough to gain my re-entry.

It was now late in the evening, and the prospect of driving several hours back to Zagreb did not appeal to me. I found a small hotel in close proximity to the border and decided enough was enough. My travel for this twenty-four-hour period had come to a full halt. Tomorrow, things would look better.

It's interesting how circumstances always feel more dire at night. This has always been true for me. With the dawn of a new day, perspective returns, and focus moves me forward with the task at hand.

After a nice breakfast, I packed my small bag and headed eastward again through Slovenia and Croatia toward the capital, Zagreb. I arrived in Zagreb midday and found a hotel. I would definitely be staying overnight until the US consulate opened Monday morning. I then spent the remainder of the day touring Zagreb's sights.

Bright and early Monday morning, I was waiting at the gate of the US consulate for it to open. Although I no longer had a passport in my possession, I was able to talk my way into the building. The American consular officer was sympathetic to my plight and immediately had an aide call the police station in eastern Croatia that had confiscated my passport. The US consulate representative made whoever answered the phone at the station aware that the US government was interested in my situation in light of my claim of mistreatment by one of their officers. Information was given to us regarding my pending court proceeding, which would apparently take place later that afternoon. When the aide to the consular hung up the phone, her comment was, "They seemed very provincial." I confirmed this from first-hand experience.

Without time to waste, I thanked the consulate staff for their assistance and headed east toward the alleged scene of the crime, Slavonski Brod. I was asked to keep the consulate informed of any further "human rights violations" that took place in my upcoming encounters with Croatian law enforcement.

Although it was not easily located, I eventually found the building in which my court proceeding was to take place. Upon showing my receipt for the confiscated passport, I was ushered into a holding area in the vicinity of the courtroom and was told to wait for a translator who would be joining me shortly. In due time, a translator stepped into the room, introduced herself, and informed me that we would be meeting the judge momentarily. Sure enough, in just a matter of minutes, I was escorted out of the holding area and into what I can only describe as one of the most spacious and impressive courtrooms I had ever seen.

My immediate thought was that this space must have been designed for communist government show trials. I was seated at what must have been the defendant's desk, and far above me, in his lofty position of authority, sat the presiding judge. As intimidating as the entire scene was to me, I also found it a bit comical, as we were the only ones in the huge expanse save for a few court clerks.

The judge began the hearing by reading the charges leveled against me. They remained the same – speeding and passing three cars illegally. After my translator repeated the indictments from the police officer to me in English, I was then asked by the judge how I would like to plead. Interestingly, until this point, my mind had been so preoccupied with all of the logistics of making it to court that I had not contemplated my answer to this question.

Now I was in a quandary. Should I tell the judge exactly what happened, or plead guilty, take my lumps, and get out of there as quickly as possible? My father has always told me that the need for justice is strong with me, and he is correct. Sometimes this need even outweighs common sense. This was one of those instances.

With the help of my translator, I told the judge exactly what had transpired during my encounter with this region's local law enforcement officers, even describing the assault. I concluded my remarks with the statement, "While I did not do any of the things for which I am accused, I am prepared to pay any fee or fine necessary to resolve this case and go home." The judge listened quietly and without any comment. He then fined me ten dollars and declared the case closed.

Ten dollars. All of this trouble and four days of wasted time, expense, and energy all for a ten-dollar bill. As I was preparing to leave the courtroom, I asked my translator if she would ask the judge how I was to recover my passport. Feeling a sense of relief that this ordeal was finally over, I was now brought back to reality when the judge responded that I would need to take the receipt for the payment of my fine to the precinct police station where my passport had been confiscated.

"Can you remind him that these are the people who physically assaulted me?" I asked my translator. She conveyed my concern to the presiding judge, and his response was that these are our procedures. Oh great. It looked like I had at least one more adventure ahead of me before this ordeal would be put to rest.

I paid my fine at the court building and asked for instructions on how to get to the police outpost that held my passport. It would be a short drive out of town. I was so ready to get this nightmare over that I did not delay in heading straight to the police station. My hope was that the officers on duty would be the same ones who had received the call from the US consulate a few hours earlier. I also anticipated that the involvement of the US government would carry a good deal of weight.

The police station turned out to be a dump in the middle of nowhere. The building was dilapidated and small. It had, at best, a maximum of six rooms in total. As I observed the facilities from the outside, I immediately understood why its officers might be in desperate need of hard currency. Who would want to work in this place?

Entering the building, the first thing I noticed was a group of officers sitting in an entry lounge chatting away as if they hadn't a care in the world. Maybe they were on break, but most likely, this was how their days were typically passed. Conversation among these officers stopped instantly the moment I stepped inside the door. I also noticed that my buddy, the offending officer, was sitting together with the group. Their recognition of me was proof in my mind that the consulate's engagement in my state of affairs had made station news. Now, let's hope it carried some influence.

To my left, I saw what looked like an information or registration counter with an officer behind it. Trying not to make eye contact with the gentlemen in the break area, I made my way to the counter. I set my receipt in front of the duty officer and simply said, "My passport, please." Now the laughter and condescending looks began from the peanut gallery across the room. It was obvious that, while they might have to cooperate with what was transpiring, there was no way that these men were going to let me leave this building without showing me their sense of disdain.

After a far too lengthy period of waiting, I finally was able to retrieve my passport that was laid on the counter and quickly made my exit. I had no eye contact with Slavonski Brod's finest, who were still milling around. As hurriedly as possible, I was in the Patrol and back on the road.

By this time, as much as I wanted to get out of Yugoslavia, it was too late in the day to travel further. I would be making no more bad decisions on this trip. I decided to make my way back to Zagreb and spend one final night in Croatia before heading home on Tuesday – four days delayed in Yugoslavia because of a ten-dollar traffic fine.

In the book of Numbers, chapter 14, Joshua and Caleb are frustrated with the Israelites for their lack of trust that God would provide for them the land that He had promised. According to the ten spies who had scouted out the territory with Joshua and Caleb, the obstacles that needed to be overcome to possess the land seemed too great.

"Joshua…and Caleb…who were among those who had explored the land, tore their clothes and said to the entire Israelite assembly, 'The land we passed through and explored is exceedingly good. If the Lord is pleased with us, he will lead us into that land, a land flowing with milk and honey, and will give it to us. Only do not rebel against the Lord and do not be afraid of the people of the land, because we will devour them. Their protection is gone, but the Lord is with us. Do not be afraid of them.'" (Numbers 14:6-9, NIV).

God had led me to this work. Just as with the children of Israel, He had already preordained the outcome of my endeavors, if only I would not fear, but rather trust in Him as my protector as Joshua and Caleb had done. These lands of Eastern Europe belonged to the Lord. They were His. The hold the enemy had on them was only temporary. It was now up to God's army, His children, to take possession of what was rightfully His with faith and action, without terror or dread.

I steered the Patrol toward home, and I thanked the Lord for the protection He had provided me. God had once again made a way for me in the midst of difficult circumstances. I was elated to finally be home. The only lasting casualty as a result of my trip was that Suzi and her family never invited me back to make up for the afternoon coffee I had missed.

CHAPTER FIVE

CONFESSIONS OF A BIBLE SMUGGLER

From the moment my plane touched down in Germany on that fall morning of 1988, I was never again to experience a problem with ulcers. Even with the countless risky endeavors I endured living in Germany and traveling in Eastern Europe over the next seven years, my ulcers never returned. The Lord equips those He calls.

Michelle and I dated long-distance that year. In the late 1980s, prior to the availability of email to the common man, maintaining a long-distance relationship was problematic. Aerograms, which were single-sheet, foldable, price-discounted letters used to transmit the written word across oceans, were our standard form of communication. Michelle and I purchased them in bulk. Also, without the internet, the telephone was our only means of verbal interaction.

International telephone calls were outrageously expensive. Michelle would call me once a week during the late evening when long-distance rates would decrease. I would receive those calls in the middle of the night due to the time difference between America and Germany. I remember many mornings waking up trying to recall if my conversation that morning with Michelle had been real or a dream. Years later, we joked that we should have invited the CEO of AT&T to our wedding. He owed us a fabulous wedding gift!

A year into my time in Germany, the summer of 1989, Michelle came for a visit with my future father-in-law, Neil. Michelle had graduated from ORU and was preparing to go to work for the public accounting firm, Price Waterhouse, in Pittsburgh. We had survived the first year apart, and we were excited to be reunited at last, albeit with a chaperone.

On a beautiful afternoon in my small town of Bergen, Germany, while climbing Englestein rock and enjoying a picnic lunch together, I proposed to Michelle. We were on the summit that overlooked the beautiful lake Chiemsee. We celebrated with a quick weekend bus tour to Venice, Italy—with Neil in tow, of course. Not many can say that they have been on a romantic Venetian gondola with their fiancée of just a few days and her father!

The week passed too quickly, and soon Michelle and I were back in our own worlds. Hers, the corporate world of accounting, and mine, a rapidly changing Eastern Europe that was about to open to the Gospel due to the collapse of the Iron Curtain.

In the fall of 1989, Mission Possible's smuggling operations became more difficult and dangerous. Some Eastern European countries, like Hungary, relaxed their tight grip on their citizens, while other more hardline nations, like Romania and Albania, tightened theirs all the more. Most of my smuggling ventures were focused on Romania, and every trip was becoming more stressful and difficult.

At the end of November, I returned from what had been a tough trip. Ceausescu's decades-long hold on Romania was beginning to weaken. Pockets of unrest and unheard-of protests were seen in isolated locations throughout the country. Cities, such as Timisoara, were starting to flex their independent muscles against the regime. Ceausescu's response was to double down on his repressive tactics in Romania.

The Romanian government was now almost completely isolated from the rest of Europe. The only program on the TV in my hotel room prior to my departure on this November trip was a documentary on the wonders of Albania, the other hardline socialist nation that was still standing shoulder-to-shoulder with Romania.

The next morning was November 30th and also my birthday. I drove across the Romanian border into Hungary, nursing a diesel engine that was full of water due to poor Romanian winter fuel supplies. As I looked for the first available gas station to top off my tank with real diesel, I sensed that the days of Romania's communist dictatorship were numbered. Little did I realize that less than a month later, on Christmas day, December 25th, 1989, Nicolae Ceausescu and his wife, Elena, would be shot dead by a Romanian firing squad for their decades of atrocities committed against the Romanian people.

The spring of 1990 was a time of transition, both for Mission Possible and for me. With the doors of freedom now opened wide throughout Eastern Europe, an organization like Mission Possible that specialized in smuggling Christian literature found itself re-evaluating its purpose. The countries that I had previously smuggled literature into

(Romania, Bulgaria, Hungary, former Yugoslavia, former Czechoslovakia) were all now open to the West. This meant my role in helping Christians in these nations would change significantly.

A new thrust of Mission Possible in Eastern Europe became leadership and pastoral training. Seminars for pastors were conducted, children and youth ministers were trained, and of course, Christian literature began to flow unhindered into these once-repressive nations. For me, this meant more travel, but without the pressure of breaking the law!

Michelle's time was occupied with her new job with Price Waterhouse in Pittsburgh and studying for the CPA exam. We continued our long-distance courtship, but it was made easier by the anticipation of a July wedding. In the pre-internet era, we made a feeble attempt at working through a premarital counseling book together. Our efforts were undoubtedly hindered by the ocean that separated us.

Michelle and I were married on July 28th, 1990, in Ouray, Colorado, in the same small Presbyterian church in which her parents had been married a quarter of a century earlier. Surrounded by wonderful family, friends, and the beautiful San Juan mountains, I felt a sense of euphoria. After two long years of separation, Michelle and I would now be together – forever. As excited as we were to get married, we would soon realize that transitioning from two years of not seeing each other to being together constantly would be easier said than done.

Having passed her CPA exams and with her year of required work for her CPA license completed, Michelle and I agreed to continue to serve with Mission Possible from the organization's German headquarters. After a quick but wonderful honeymoon in San Francisco, and with only a few weeks of marriage under our belts, Michelle and I excitedly boarded a plane to Germany to start our life of mission work together.

To say that we hit the ground running is an understatement. There were adjustments required from both of us to be happily married, and privacy was also a problem. Michelle and I calculated that we had visitors staying with us approximately seventy percent of our first year of marriage. Our office and apartment were located in the same building, so there were times that we had to go downstairs into the office to work out disagreements.

Those initial challenges so often faced by young married couples were offset by the excitement we experienced being able to travel together throughout both Western and Eastern Europe. It was an amazing time of serving the Lord as a couple and visiting many new destinations.

Mission Possible had now appointed me as their European Director. I was responsible for the organization's European programming, including its two offices – one in Bergen, Germany, and the other in Helsinki, Finland. Michelle took the role of overseeing the organization's European finances, a job that, with her training, she did exceedingly well.

In the fall of 1990, I was twenty-six years of age. I had been placed in a demanding leadership role. I not only sensed that I was inadequately prepared for these new responsibilities, but I also felt intimidated. Most of those with whom I worked were significantly older. One trip, in particular, challenged me to my core. I had traveled to a remote area of Siberia in the former Soviet Union to meet with a large team of church planters Mission Possible was supporting. Sitting down with this group of men who had given up every creature comfort in order to serve the Lord as missionaries in this frozen corner of the globe, I felt woefully inadequate. Spiritually, I felt like a lightweight. I also understood that, as a young man, I had not accomplished anything to earn their respect or the right to lead them.

Feelings of inadequacy amidst the significant responsibilities that were thrust upon me caused me to stumble through my early years of leadership. As I could do nothing about my age, I focused on the authority that had been given me to do the job. Rather than team building or serving those I led, I used my authority to get the desired results I wanted to achieve. While I would not describe my leadership style as dictatorial, I did not model servant leadership to those with whom I co-labored.

After the collapse of the communist government in Romania, Albania remained one of the last vestiges of true communism in Europe. After all of the recent events in Eastern Europe, it was apparent to most observers that the question was not if Albania would open to the West, but when that would take place. Because of this, Christian mission agencies had been meeting for some time in England in the hope of coordinating efforts to evangelize Albania when that door opened. The group called itself the Albanian Encouragement Project, or AEP, and its noble goal of entering Albania together, as united mission agencies working with an integrated purpose, was being planned during its periodic meetings in London.

Michelle and I began to attend these meetings as representatives of Mission Possible. Once again, we found ourselves as some of the youngest attendees at these gatherings. It was interesting to hear about all of the "cracks" that were developing in the Albanian government's wall of isolation. On a limited basis, British tourist trips had already been allowed to visit the country. But now, even humanitarian aid shipments were occasionally reaching Albania. Almost every month, there was a new story of an organization's unexpected ability to access this tiny nation for the first time. I began to pray about how Mission Possible might one day be able to work in Albania, the Land of the Eagles.

In the early months of 1991, I felt impressed by the Holy Spirit to write a letter to the history department of the University of Tirana that was located in Albania's capital city. Having studied history and US government at ORU with earned teaching credentials, I asked the university if there might be a possibility for Michelle and me to visit their institution as a cultural exchange of sorts. I posted that letter in the cold winter months of early 1991, and then let it slip from my mind. In late spring, a type-written letter, obviously from a typewriter of an era gone by, arrived at our German office.

I was floored by its contents. Inside was a personal invitation from the head of the History Department of the University of Tirana, Dr. Paskal Milo, inviting Michelle and me to visit. Dr. Milo instructed us to contact the Albanian embassy in Germany to arrange our visas, and once that process was complete, we would be free to make our travel preparations to visit Albania. Michelle and I were in a state of shock in regard to this news. Albania was a restricted country, and at that time, few individuals from the West had been allowed to visit. Americans were especially unwelcome by the Albanian government. There was no question that this invitation was a miracle.

As I began to communicate with the Albanian ambassador to Germany regarding our visas, Michelle and I were in for an additional surprise. Within weeks of receiving our invitation to Albania, we were informed that Dr. Milo had been appointed to the position of the Minister of Education in the Albanian government. We were no longer traveling to Albania to see a history professor at the University of Tirana, but to meet Albania's new Minister of Education!

One of the most memorable events of my life was our plane touching down at the Rinas airport just outside of Tirana that hot summer day in late June 1991. We were received at the airport by one of the university's history professors, Petrit (Peter) Nathanaili, whose family would later become close friends of ours. After being warmly welcomed, we were taken to the Hotel Tirana, which was in the center of downtown. Once we had checked into our non-airconditioned room on one of the upper floors of this high-rise, we joined Peter at the hotel's balcony restaurant for a refreshing evening drink at the conclusion of what had been a very hot summer day.

One of the first things we noticed while driving the twenty minutes from the airport to the hotel was the complete absence of cars. We were one of the only vehicles on the road. As we casually chatted with Peter at the hotel while getting acquainted, he informed us that the private ownership of cars had just been legalized in Albania during the past few months. Michelle and I began to realize that the short Swiss Air flight we had taken to this tiny Balkan land was really a time machine that had transported us back to a different age, one with which we were not at all familiar.

Peter began to share with us our itinerary for what was to be just short of two weeks in Albania. The next day we would meet with the faculty at the University of Tirana, followed by a meeting with Dr. Milo, who was now the Minister of Education. Those aspects of our itinerary were expected, but what Peter told us next blew our minds.

Following our time with Dr. Milo and his faculty, we would be given a car, a chauffeur, a translator, and a history professor as a guide to tour the nation at the full expense of the Albanian government. Coming from our Western culture where money was always an issue, we found ourselves in an emerging, post-communist culture where power and influence carried the same weight as money. Apparently, every door had just been opened for us.

It is difficult to describe the journey that unfolded over the next days: roadways devoid of vehicles other than our own, shepherds taking naps in the road almost getting hit because they were not expecting cars, some of the most beautiful scenery we had ever experienced, military bunker upon bunker dotting the hillsides ready for an American invasion, spikes on the support posts of every vineyard in place to impale the invading imperialist paratroopers, and goats in trees. The entire expedition was dream-like. All the while, we had a university professor explaining the rich and remarkable historical background of everything we were experiencing.

Upon the conclusion of our journey, which took us through much of the country, we had a few days remaining in Tirana. The extraordinary hospitality of Albanians was evident by all of the invitations we received to visit the homes of those who had hosted us during our stay. We became especially close to the Nathanaili household, and we were intrigued by the stories of the family's communist past in the Albanian diplomatic service. Of particular interest were photo albums with pictures of the matriarch, Cleopatra, and her late husband posed with the "gang of four" in Mao Zedong's China. Most interesting of all to us in these photographs were the faces of their Albanian colleagues who had fallen out of favor with the communist Albanian government. Their faces had been "erased" from the images as if they had never existed.

On the final evening before our departure, Dr. Milo arranged a reception for us in the dining room of one of Tirana's most historic hotels, the Hotel Dajti. (Several years later, Michelle and I would see Mother Teresa, who was ethnically Albanian, at this same hotel.) The evening was wonderful, with good food, new friends, and lots of laughing and smiles. It was the perfect conclusion to an incredible trip. As the evening wound down, Paskal asked me to make some concluding remarks. This was the moment for which I had prepared. It was my opportunity to speak hope, life, and Christ into this nation.

I don't precisely remember what I said that evening, but I do remember emphasizing that after years of communism in Albania, their nation needed to be rebuilt upon a foundation of God and His spiritual principles. Pointing the Albanians to the path of freedom through Christ Jesus was the reason Michelle and I had come to Albania.

When I sat down following my remarks, and Dr. Milo began to make his concluding address, I was concerned that I might have overstepped some unknown boundary in this public forum. But those fears were soon put to rest when Paskal not only thanked us for coming but asked us to return with whatever tools we could bring to help rebuild this biblical foundation of which I had spoken. Closing words such as these were beyond what we could have hoped to have heard.

The next day, Peter and his family drove Michelle and me to the Rinas airport, where our Albanian adventure had begun. The family was delighted with the short excursion, as the children had never seen an airplane and had rarely ridden in a car. Our goodbyes were joyful, as we were excited to have made such wonderful new friends. We also knew that this would be the first of many trips to this amazing land. So, with a final wave goodbye, off we flew aboard our Swiss Air time machine to our German home, returning to Western Europe, land of plenty.

Politically, the proverbial dam broke in Albania during the summer and fall of 1991. The Albanian Encouragement Project was able to conduct the first evangelism rally in the Tirana soccer stadium that summer and the new converts from this event became the backbone of the fledgling Albanian church. Albania was now officially open to the rest of the world.

Following our June trip, Mission Possible began to emphasize work in Albania as an organizational priority. Over the next several years, Michelle and I would make numerous journeys back and forth to Tirana. Leadership training seminars were conducted, mission teams were sent, and humanitarian aid was delivered. A Mission Possible office was even opened in that nation thanks to the help of Besa Shapllo, MP's new Albanian Director.

My father and mother traveled from the US to join me on a trip to Albania in those early days. One day during our stay, as I was taking care of other organizational business in town, Dad visited the public schools in Tirana. During that visit, he met a woman named Besa, who invited my parents to her home. Besa and my parents became instant friends. Before we left Tirana for home, Dad shared the Gospel message with her. Besa immediately accepted the redemptive gift of Jesus Christ. God had been working in her heart for many years preparing her for that day of being introduced to the salvation story – Besa was ready!

Over the next few years, Michelle and I had the privilege of working with Besa and her husband, Agron, to help establish an official presence for Mission Possible in Albania. Once the organization's registration with the government was complete, we were told that it was the second officially recognized nonprofit organization in Albania's history. Mother Teresa's Missionaries of Charity had been the first.

It was during these exciting days of rapid ministry growth in Albania that the Mann family was growing as well. Weathering an initial scare that required a short period of bed rest for Michelle, on May 2, 1993, William Andrew Mann was welcomed into the world. Michelle and I will always remember with joy and laughter the challenges of having a baby while living in a foreign country.

During the days following Andrew's birth, I continued my heavy travel schedule throughout Eastern Europe. Unfortunately, Michelle carried the brunt of taking care of Andrew alone as he grew into a toddler. There were lots of happy family times with us often traveling together. Even as a baby, Andrew was a great traveler.

Besa began establishing one of the first nonprofit offices in Albania while at the same time working to launch the Christian children's magazine, Miracle, which was sponsored by both Mission Possible and the Christian Broadcasting Network (CBN). Over the next few years, Miracle Magazine successfully spread across the country with children's clubs being established in many of the major cities of Albania. Together with CBN, Albanian television began to broadcast Christian programming, which now became a part of Besa's new work. During those early days of work in Albania, our activities were exciting. Everything felt new, and the sky seemed the limit in regard to what we could try in order to reach Albania for Christ.

While the new opportunities for Mission Possible in Albania thrilled me, my job continued to require much of my focus to be placed on other countries in Eastern Europe where Mission Possible was engaged. This meant that I was traveling more than ever, including periodic trips to the US for meetings with the US office leadership.

With the transformational changes that had taken place in Eastern Europe, my father and the Mission Possible board of directors were also contemplating major changes for the organization. One of those changes that was discussed in 1994 was the closing of our office in Germany. Having been intimately involved in both the construction and establishment of the office only a few years earlier, the topic of closing our German facility came as quite a shock to me. I thought it was a bad idea.

I had many emotions when it came to closing the German office, but I also knew that I had sound arguments in regard to my objections. After months of uncertainty, the leadership of MP decided to close the office in Germany and sell the facilities. It was further agreed that after the sale and closure of the office, which I would oversee, I would then be offered the position of Vice President of Operations in the States. The handwriting was on the wall. Michelle and I were not ready for this change, nor were we happy about it, but we were leaving Europe.

The latter months of 1994 were difficult for Michelle and me. Not only was the sale and closure of the German office challenging, but the prospect of leaving all of our German friends of so many years and starting a new life in the US was daunting and unwanted. The one bright spot in all of the turmoil was discovering that Michelle was pregnant. A few months later, as we were neck-deep in closing the office, selling the building, and preparing for our return to the US, we discovered that we were awaiting a beautiful baby girl.

It was with much sadness and fond memories that in the summer of 1995, we said goodbye to our close friends in Germany. As we left, Michelle, Andrew, and I made one final stop at our office in Finland before arriving in Dallas for what would soon become several years that were mixed with joy and difficulty.

The joy came quickly in the birth of our second child, Abigail Grace Mann, who was born in early November. It was wonderful to have lots of family present as we welcomed Abby into the world. Andrew, who wanted to name the new baby Tummy Button Mann, was the only one who wasn't happy with the new arrival. However, he soon adapted to his change in circumstances.

Many aspects of our return to the US were difficult, and adjusting to living in the US was a struggle. Michelle was now taking care of two small children in our rental home while I went to the office on a daily basis. This was a significant change for us. In all our prior years of ministry, our work had always been a partnership. Finding a new church was not easy either, and trying to fit into the routine of the US office regimen challenged me. Michelle and I both recognized that we were missing the European culture and lifestyle to which we had grown accustomed over the previous five years.

We both tried our best to "establish roots" and prove to the Mission Possible organization that we were team players, despite our feelings of being fish out of water. We purchased a house, joined a local church, and did our best to settle into our new roles as they related to both work and family.

No matter how hard Michelle and I tried to adjust to life in America, there was a yearning in our hearts to be overseas. We continued to feel that our time on the mission field had been ended abruptly, terminated prematurely, against our will and better judgment. These feelings made it difficult to find peace and contentment in our new environment.

My time working in the US office in close proximity with my father was proving to be more complicated than I had anticipated. Differing management styles put us often at odds with one another. Where an ocean had previously separated our working relationship, we were now separated only by an office wall.

I believe that there are three types of father/son business relationships. One – fathers and sons who can easily work together. Two – fathers and sons who could never work together under any circumstance. Three – fathers and sons who can work together, but probably shouldn't. Dad and I fit this last category. As 1996 drew to a close, it became apparent that my time of working with my father and for Mission Possible was coming to an end.

But what next? I felt more adrift than ever regarding the future that the Lord had for both my family and me. As Michelle and I began to pray for open doors, we were unprepared for the adventure God had before us.

For the last several years, Michelle and I had watched get-rich-quick pyramid schemes take hold in Albania. Many of our close Albanian friends had invested their life savings in these too good to be true money-making opportunities that had no governmental oversight. In January of 1997, with the collapse of the largest of these schemes, including one of the most popular, VEFA, the country descended into chaos. By March of that year, much of the army and police force in Albania had deserted, and a state of anarchy existed. Most Western missionaries and foreign nationals had evacuated the country. The Albanian Encouragement Project that Michelle and I had worked hard to help create now stored the contents of its Albanian office in a shipping container as the office expatriate staff had fled the country.

Michelle and I watched the events that were unfolding in Albania in disbelief. It appeared to us that all of the hard work that the missionary community had done over the last few years was now being wholly undone in a chaotic national rage. As our fellow in-country missionaries were evacuated by their US and British governments, we had a hard time comprehending that the Albania we loved was now dramatically changing.

More surprising was the telephone call we received late spring from one of the AEP board members. The board was requesting that Michelle and I move with our young family to Albania to reopen the AEP office. It was explained to us that missionaries were expected to start returning to the country in early 1998 and that the AEP administrative structure needed to be functioning by that time in order to facilitate their re-entry. I would manage the AEP office as the Administrator, and Michelle would oversee the organization's finances. Surprised by the offer, Michelle and I agreed to pray and get back to the AEP board with a decision.

By this time, I was sure that I needed to leave Mission Possible. However, leaving our new home that we had recently purchased and the new relationships we had worked so hard to develop was another story. The thought of bringing my young family into what was now a war zone in Albania had very little appeal to me. But we did pray, and in very short order, both Michelle and I knew that returning to Albania, this time to live as a family, was what we needed to do.

This decision to return to Albania to live set into motion a whirlwind of events. First, our departure from Mission Possible was finalized. With the board's blessing, I was cleared to leave employment with MP the coming fall. While I had my ups and downs working with my father, I was truly blessed by the experience. The opportunities that were afforded me in my ten years of employment with both my father and Mission Possible were invaluable, and they would set the course for the remainder of my life's journey. I was looking forward to rekindling a father-son relationship with Dad that was void of business dealings. For now, though, new undertakings lay ahead.

Immediately, the formidable task of selling our newly acquired home got underway. This task deflated our spirits. The AEP board wanted us to report to Europe by late fall. We were to attend an AEP board meeting in Corfu, Greece, and then arrive in Albania prior to the end of the year. This meant that tickets would have to be purchased by the end of the summer.

As the weeks flew by, our anxiety grew in regard to the prospects of selling our home. With only a few house showings having taken place, it was apparent that a miracle was going to be required to get us out of Texas. In order to save money for a family of four, we had purchased our airline tickets for Greece well in advance. Our departure date was set in stone for mid-fall with no wiggle room. But the house was an issue.

Early in the sale process, our realtor had asked that if anyone randomly came to the door to see the house, we should tell them to contact the realtor for an appointment. To date, this had not happened. One Saturday afternoon, the doorbell rang. A couple wanted to look at the house. Obedient to our realtor's wishes, I informed them that they should contact our realtor to schedule an appointment. The couple politely agreed and walked away.

When I returned to the kitchen, Michelle asked me who had been at the door. I mentioned the couple and my instructions to them. Her next statement was along the lines of, "Are you crazy?" We had been living for months in a perfectly clean house—even with two small children—ready at a moment's notice for a showing and no prospects of an interested party on the horizon, and I had just turned away a couple who seemed interested. A fast learner, I rushed out the front door to see if I could track them down. I caught them as they were preparing to get into their car. I profusely apologized and asked them if they would like to come in to see the house.

The couple agreed, they came in and looked around for no more than ten minutes while Michelle, the kids, and I remained in the kitchen. It was a short visit, and they politely thanked us and were gone – in the blink of an eye. The visit had been so short that Michelle and I were convinced that what we had just experienced was another disappointment.

Michelle and I continued to make preparations for our departure to Europe as if the sale of the house was not a concern. A moving company was hired to put our household items into storage, boxes were packed, and all loose ends were tied up – except the house. Prayer for the sale of our house, which had previously been one of many concerns, now became our most urgent need.

A week after our unexpected house visitation, I received a call from our realtor who had received an offer on our house. The agent was confused, however, as they had no record of having shown the home to this potential buyer. While the offer was less than what we were asking, it was well within our margin of flexibility. The couple who had visited us that weekend purchased our home based on a ten-minute inspection without a second look. Closing documentation was signed three days before we boarded our non-refundable flight to Europe.

Following several days of meetings in Corfu, we visited our good friends, Bob and Hanne Wittenzellner, in Germany. Bob and Hanne graciously allowed us to stay with them for several weeks while we prepared for our final push into Albania. With the Christmas season quickly approaching, we were anxious to get on our way and settled in our new home country. Anticipating the need for a car in Albania, we had shipped ours from the US to Europe.

It was a gloomy winter day when we picked up our vehicle near Bob and Hanne's home in Traunstein, Germany. Shortly thereafter, our road journey began, taking us through Austria and Italy to our final Western European stop in Trieste. From there, it was onto an Italian ferry with its port of debarkation Durres, Albania.

As our American-made sedan rolled off the ferry a day later with Abby's tricycle mounted on the roof, we realized, by looking at the mass of humanity swarming the Albanian port, that our young family was in for an adventure.

CHAPTER SIX
KYRIE ELEISON - ALBANIA

We arrived in Tirana just weeks before Christmas. Our prayer was that the Lord would have mercy on our young family's new beginning in Albania. Missionary friends, Erik and Joanna Stensland, were kind enough to open their home to us for several weeks while we searched for an adequate place to live, which was not easy in Tirana. Most homes available for rent were either dilapidated, without reliable running water and electricity, or too expensive at rates that were inflated by the presence of the expatriate community. When inspecting homes for rent, I was warned that finding a bathtub filled with water was never a good sign as it indicated a poor water supply. We had the good fortune of finding a house that perfectly suited our small family's needs, almost in the center of the city, on Tefta Tasko road. Many missionaries who returned to Albania from their time away after having been evacuated were envious of our accommodations. They were sparse by American standards, but a wonderful find in Albania.

The year was 1998, and our little family attempted to adjust to life in Albania. Daily power and water outages were the norm, and the crack of AK-47s in the streets outside our window put us to sleep each night. This became a part of our daily routine.

We found ingenious ways to cope, thanks in part to the advice of other, more seasoned missionaries in Tirana. Our problem with a lack of water was resolved when we installed two storage tanks for when the municipal water supply did not function. One of these tanks was on the ground level of our home and would begin to suck water from the city pipes as soon as the water started flowing – provided I remembered to turn on the pump. It would then pump water up to a second reservoir that I had installed on our roof. It served two functions. First, it was an additional storage container for our much-needed water supply, and second, it would gravity-feed water into the house during our frequent extended hours of no electricity when pumps wouldn't work. Because of this, as long as we conserved our water usage, we had a consistent supply of water. Mike Jeffries, my old college roommate who was the mission pastor at First Baptist Church in Ft. Lauderdale, Florida, which supported us as missionaries, purchased a power inverter for us that helped immensely with the frequent electrical outages.

When we had been in the new house for about a month, we were visited by a representative of the centralized Albanian power company. Apparently, our electrical usage was measured as "off the charts" by Albanian standards. Since we often tripped electrical breakers by running one too many appliances, I was quite certain that their meter reading was accurate. Trying to explain this to the power company representative was a fun cross-cultural experience.

Days were damp, dark, and cold during our first winter in Tirana. While temperatures never fell below freezing, with no heat in homes, everything seemed to stay cold. Rudimentary propane heaters were what gave us warmth in the house since too many electric heaters would overload the circuit breakers. Much of our available free time was spent securing household provisions for either sustenance or warmth. Surviving required much of our daily energy, and I was convinced that the propane heaters were killing us with their fumes.

Living in Tirana during 1998 and 1999 was a bit like stepping back in time. Because of the instability of the government and civil society, many of the things that governments organize in a normal, well-functioning metropolitan area either functioned very poorly or did not function at all. Trash collection was a big problem, and garbage would pile up on the streets until something would have to be done. This led to other issues such as rats, stray animals, and disease. A multitude of unintended consequences was the result of the city's inability to collect the garbage.

In regard to the urban infrastructure, power and water were just the tip of the iceberg when it came to the government's failings. Most streets were in need of repair, with many potholes so large that you could lose your car in one. It was also not uncommon to fall into an open manhole on the sidewalk at night. Few of the city's streetlights worked, and many of the manhole covers were missing entirely. We had brought an umbrella stroller with us from the US for two-year-old Abby, but it was practically useless. What was really needed was some kind of baby all-terrain vehicle.

All of this was a result of Albania's embrace of communism decades earlier. Pioneered in part by 19th century Karl Marx, communism was the theory of the common ownership of all wealth. In a pure communist society, which has never existed, this would include the common ownership of all economic enterprise and property. In true communism, the individual sacrificed his or her rights for the betterment of the collective good. Communism was embraced by Albania following the collapse of the Axis powers at the end of WWII in the mid-1940s.

In the former Soviet Union, which was a strong ally of Albania in the early years of Albania's communist government, a new form of communism emerged. It was called Marxist-Leninism, and it was a hybrid philosophy of one of the Soviet Union's first heads of state, Vladimir Lenin, and the ideas of Karl Marx. In the Soviet Union, Christianity was repressed as it challenged the allegiance of the citizenry to the State. It was not abnormal in Soviet schools for elementary children to be taught that there was no God and to be asked to inform on their parents if Christianity was taught in their home. In the classroom, children would be asked to pray to God for ice cream. When none would be forthcoming, the youngsters then would be instructed to pray to father Lenin for the same thing – and the ice cream would be wheeled into the room. From this example, children were taught that the Soviet Communist State would provide for their every need throughout life. The nation of Albania embraced this concept in spades, even breaking their alliance with the Soviet Union in 1956 in order to align with the more hardline communist government of China.

Our family was now living through the ramifications of the complete collapse of Albanian communism. We experienced a good example of how utterly broken the Albanian system had become one day when our telephone line went dead. After checking with the telephone company to see if they could send a repairman to resolve our issue, I was informed that it would take a year before the next technician would be available to visit our home. However, I was also told if I would like to contact the repairman personally, he would be more than happy to come over after hours – for an appropriate fee, of course. This was the new, unregulated free market that was in direct conflict with the old communist system.

In the days when communism ruled, individual thought or individual initiative was not celebrated. People were told what to do and when to do it. On election day, for example, people were told how early they needed to show up to the local polling venue in order to cast their vote for the only candidate on the ticket – the dictator, Enver Hoxha. It wasn't enough for someone to vote the party line; they were also required to line up early in order to prove their enthusiasm for the autocrat. This train of thought had trickled down over the years into every aspect of society.

Most people living in Tirana lived in block housing complexes. In the past, if a family lived in one of these, there would be a compulsory "communal cleaning day," where everyone, whether they wanted to or not, would be required to assist in cleaning the building. College students would have mandatory government service projects in addition to their studies, which might include assignments for both men and women, such as helping to rebuild or maintain the nation's railroad.

Living through decades of such oppression, it was only logical that citizens were now rebelling from forced social engagement. Here is how far society had deteriorated: in the Tirana of 1997, you could walk through one of the most trash-filled, filthy streets in the city to visit a friend's house, and once inside the walls of their small home, you would find everything tidy and in beautiful order. What lay outside of their walled compound was simply someone else's responsibility. That someone else, which was the government, didn't work.

As disturbing as all of this was for a creature of order like me, these difficulties were just minor inconveniences in comparison to Albania's real problem of governmental instability. The fact that the new democratically elected institutions of power were so weak and ineffective led to major security issues for the residents of Albania. Crime was out of control, and after the nation's armories had been looted in early 1997, guns flooded the country. Everyone had a gun – both the good guys and the bad guys. The problem was that there no longer remained a well-functioning law enforcement system to help distinguish the good from the bad. What resulted was a level of societal chaos that few in Western nations have been forced to experience.

Of course, these were simply a few of the challenges that confronted us as we attempted to root ourselves in Tirana. At the same time, Michelle and I started work at the office of the Albanian Encouragement Project (AEP). The two of us were tasked with reopening the AEP. It had been closed during the majority of the previous year while most of the missionaries had been evacuated from the country. I was given the challenge of upgrading the organization in regard to the services it provided to the missionaries, and Michelle was to see that the financial structure of the AEP was improved.

Missionaries slowly began to return to Albania throughout 1998. Michelle and I, working with our small staff of both missionary volunteers and paid nationals, made sure that the AEP was ready to welcome them with open arms upon their arrival. Previously, the AEP had offered missionaries a secure way of receiving mail from around the world through the assistance of Missionary Aviation Fellowship (MAF). We worked to resuscitate this mail distribution pipeline that would first see post transit through Zurich, Switzerland, before being sent to our office in Albania, where each missionary family had a mailbox.

In previous years, a lending library had been created to loan both books and videos to missionaries and their families when they visited Tirana from the various outlying regions of the country. This proved to be a popular service, especially for families with small children. An enhancement to our library that we created involved the newly emerging internet. In Albania, internet access was still new, and no internet cafés existed. A service we offered our members was a work terminal connected to the web that was housed in the AEP office.

I developed another service that was of assistance to most AEP members. Working with the Albanian Foreign Ministry, I created a system whereby all missionaries who were members of the AEP could apply for their Albanian residency visas through our AEP office. Now, members were no longer required to spend untold hours running from ministry to ministry trying to get their papers in order for their families to live in the country. Not only was this a time-saver for the missionaries, but it streamlined the process of securing residency visas for the government. The new system was infinitely more efficient than the previous process. Of course, this did create a mountain of additional work and logistical challenges for the AEP staff, but, after all, that was part of our job as a facilitating umbrella organization.

One final task in getting the office restructured was improving how our AEP national meetings were organized. I worked to create a method that would allow us to cooperate as organizations more efficiently. Additionally, the new structure helped member organizations avoid duplicating efforts.

This was hard work, especially in the Albanian context, where nothing happened easily. Nevertheless, Michelle and I had much success in our reorganization of the AEP. By the time we left Albania, the AEP represented over seventy independent organizations, and hundreds of missionaries spread throughout the country with a fine-tuned and well-operating administrative structure.

These new systems, procedures, and structures were set up none too soon. In the spring of 1998, Albania's northern neighbor, Kosovo, became engulfed in a war with Serbia. As springtime moved into summer in Albania, it became apparent that Albania would be caught in this conflict, primarily as a safe haven for Kosovo's Muslim refugee community that poured over the border. Quickly working together with the Albanian Evangelical Alliance, the AEP began gearing up to assist in this developing crisis.

With the assistance of groups like Tear Fund in the United Kingdom, the AEP was able to create a crisis center to deal with relief efforts that would be coordinated through the AEP. The AEP Crisis Center quadrupled the size of the AEP administrative staff and greatly expanded the AEP's budget. Now having the financial support for this developing refugee crisis arriving from around the world, the AEP's budget exploded from under one hundred thousand dollars to well over a million. Thankfully, Michelle's restructuring of the AEP financial system was ready to handle the large influx of donations.

The beginning of the war in Kosovo made things busy for the young Mann family. With a winter in Albania under our belts, Michelle and I were beginning to feel like seasoned missionaries, even though we still had much to learn. The two of us started private Albanian language lessons, although Michelle seemed to be the only one who was really benefiting from our weekly class with Rosa. With everything happening in our lives, I was much too busy, or maybe lazy, to study. Rosa was far too polite to force me to do my homework. Fortunately for our family, Michelle paid close attention and mastered the Albanian language enough to keep us well fed. I, on the other hand, relied heavily on the AEP office staff to cover my shortcomings when it came to speaking "Shqip."

The kids adjusted well to Albanian life. Because of the long hours required of both Michelle and me at the AEP office, we found a nanny for Andrew and Abby. Ornela, a young Albanian in her early twenties, quickly stole our hearts and became a member of our extended family. The kids absolutely adored her, and we trusted her completely with their care. We would often come home in the afternoons excited to hear about their daily exploits around town. To this day, Abby remains traumatized from some sort of interaction with a clown and a balloon at a circus Ornela had taken them to visit. We never figured out what happened to two-year-old Abby, but clowns and "popping noises" became family lore.

The economy in Albania also afforded us a housekeeper, and due to the large amount of dust and dirt everywhere, Victoria was a godsend. She would dust the house once a day only to have to do it again the next morning. Since Ornela was young, Victoria, who was an older woman, provided some added stability in our home when we were absent. Her advice to Michelle in the realm of how and where to shop was invaluable. We were blessed to have found Victoria.

Andrew was now five and spent his afternoons in our walled-in backyard building roads and paths with the billions of rocks that had been left by our landlord in our grassless compound; our budding civil engineer. Both Andrew and Abby discovered the joy of picking and eating "beanies," what they called the unripened green plums from our many fruit trees in the yard. When it rained, on went the galoshes and little else as the two kids splashed around in the yard for hours on end, playing together. A special summertime Saturday afternoon treat as the Albanian temperatures spiked would be a family trip up Dajti Mountain to an upscale hotel that had a swimming pool. For a few dollars each, we could enjoy a snack and have a swim in a beautiful pool that overlooked Tirana. Picnics on Dajti Mountain with Besa and Agron Shapllo were also a summer highlight.

In contrast to the fun we experienced, those summer skies were also dotted with NATO fighters returning to their base in Italy after completing their bombing missions over Kosovo, reminding us of the times in which we were living. At home, Andrew would have problems breathing when he caught a virus, a condition that was later diagnosed as RAD, or Reactive Airways Disease. We spent many evenings with him using a nebulizer and calming him down to stabilize his breathing. Walks in the middle of the night and the cool evening temperatures of Tirana were helpful for him. A fear of mine was that Andrew would have an episode during one of our numerous power outages when we would be unable to use his nebulizer. Although we did have some scary moments with his RAD, this scenario never materialized. Thankfully, Andrew did eventually outgrow this condition.

Two-year-old Abby was simply precocious, and we had a difficult time keeping up with her. The always efficient Michelle, when it came time to potty-train Abby, decided to tackle both Abby and the new puppy, Toby, at once. A top hit during 1998 was "Barbie Girl" by the group Aqua, and it was played loudly in most stores throughout Tirana. One of the atrocious lines in the song went like this, "Come on, Barbie, let's go party." At the same time, Barney the Dinosaur was a popular children's television program. Abby combined her potty-training experience with her dearly loved TV show and sang, "Come on, Barney, let's go potty."

We soon realized that bringing the car from the US to Albania had been a mistake. Michelle and I had purchased our car only a short time before our decision to move to Albania. Knowing we could never recover our investment by selling it before we left the US, I made the decision to bring it with us to Albania and sell it in Tirana. I had made the incorrect assumption that prices for such a Western product in Albania would be much higher than what we would receive for it in the US. What I did not realize at the time, however, was that a large percentage of the cars on the road in Albania were stolen vehicles, smuggled into the country from other parts of Europe. This, of course, deflated prices for used cars to the point that our Ford became, for the purpose of resale, worthless.

We had no choice but to hold onto it. We occasionally drove it to the grocery store and home, and we eventually shipped it back to America when it was time for us to return to the States. While we did not go out in it often because of fear of theft or vandalism, it was an adventure when we would take it for a drive. On one occasion, we were saluted by two police officers as we passed them in our flashy Western car with Texas license plates. I'm sure they assumed we were members of the US diplomatic corps. Once, we returned from shopping to where we had parked in downtown Tirana only to find the two boys we had paid to look after it jumping up and down on its hood.

Even while living in a place like Albania, one attempts to find normalcy in the midst of chaos. Albania's political stability was not improving; in fact, the situation was quite the opposite. Security was still a concern across the country. There were entire regions of Albania, including the north of the country and cities like Lazarat in the south, that were "no go" zones due to clan violence. Even so, everyone tried to carry on life as normal. Young American missionaries would occasionally babysit in the evenings for Michelle and me so that we could enjoy a night together out on the town. It was not unusual for us to hear gunfire while walking home from our date. On one occasion, a bomb exploded just down the street from where we were eating.

I remember sometimes being awakened in the middle of the night with a sense of panic by a recorded phone call from the security firm protecting the AEP office. "Emergency, Emergency – break-in at the AEP office" would be barked over the phone line in Albanian. I dreaded those solitary walks to the office in order to confront an intruder at 2:00 am, only to find curtains blowing in the night breeze from a window that had been left open by a staff member.

This was the climate in which Andrew was to start kindergarten in the fall of 1998. He would attend the Qiriazi School, an international missionary school, located on the outskirts of Tirana. We were excited to have him interacting with other children his age on a daily basis, and he was happy with the idea of starting school. However, our plans were delayed as Andrew's first week of school was canceled due to a failed coup attempt in the Albanian government.

Around this time, my mother was scheduled to arrive for a visit. In retrospect, she won the award for poor timing, as her visit was to start on the first day of the unrest. As the coup attempt unfolded, most places of business closed, and people locked themselves inside their homes, safely behind doors. But not me–I headed out of town to pick my mother up at the airport.

Nani, my driver at the AEP, insisted on going along. We received information from the airport that Mom's flight was still scheduled to land. We also had news that bandits were now on the roadway between Tirana and the Rinas airport randomly stopping and robbing cars. For this reason, Nani was unwavering in his insistence to accompany me. Out of an abundance of caution, our trip took much longer than was normal. Several times we were required to pull over to the side of the road as oncoming cars warned us of danger up ahead. Eventually, we made it to Rinas.

When I arrived at the airport, we were greeted with a chaotic sight. Scores of people were streaming out of the airport and getting into vehicles to leave the area as quickly as possible. Gone were those folks simply milling around or trying to convince you to hire them as a taxi service. Everyone was hell-bent on getting away as quickly as possible.

Mom's flight had not landed. We sat and waited as the parking lot grew emptier by the minute. When we arrived, I had noticed a contingency from the US embassy. I approached the head of security for the group, identified myself as an American, and asked if he could enlighten me as to the situation that was transpiring. He informed me that his delegation was waiting for the arrival of a diplomat, presumably on the same flight as my mother. He also confirmed that fighting was breaking out all along the roadways, even in Tirana, and that travel back to the capital was extremely dangerous. He stated that they would be departing just as soon as they could secure their VIP guest.

I mentioned to the embassy representative that my mother was most likely arriving on the same flight as his diplomat. I also told him that after his update, I was concerned that the two of us, both American citizens, would now be stranded. I respectfully requested that our van be allowed to join his convoy of vehicles to Tirana. He readily agreed and told me to be prepared to depart. He assured me that he would inform me when it was time to pull out.

Feeling greatly relieved, I went back to the van and informed Nani of our new arrangement. Having just lived through the harrowing experience of getting to the airport, he, too, was pleased with these new developments. While we were waiting for Mom to arrive, a lost and confused individual approached our vehicle to inquire as to the situation going on around us. He was a CNN reporter who had just arrived. He had been sent to report on the Kosovo crisis but had absolutely no idea what was happening amidst the chaos. I brought him up to speed on the events of the day and offered him a ride into town since, without it, he would be facing a difficult predicament. He gratefully accepted my kindness.

All at once, we noticed a flurry of activity at the airport exit. An evacuation of all employees had either just been ordered or was taking place because people were too afraid to stay any longer. Whichever the case, the results were the same – the airport facilities were now almost vacant. It was just us, the embassy convoy, and a few lone stragglers.

At that moment, Mom could be seen exiting the terminal. I quickly greeted her, swooped up her bags, and ushered her to the van as expeditiously as possible. Mom was completely uninformed as to what was transpiring around her, and she seemed oblivious to it all. She was simply happy to be in Albania. I tried my best to explain our dire situation, but my narrative was interrupted as I witnessed the US embassy convoy pulling out of the parking lot without us.

I jumped out of our van, ran to the convoy that was beginning to roll, and yelled to the embassy representative who had promised to take us with them. "Hey, what about us?" He responded that they had been given a new assignment and were no longer allowed to assist us–and off his team went. We now sat in an empty parking lot as the sun began to drop low in the sky.

I was both scared and angry. I was scared that we might not be able to get back to Tirana this evening and that we could be required to defend ourselves at the airport. I was angry that I had been given what I considered a commitment of protection from a United States government representative, and that protection had just driven off into the sunset.

Fortunately, over the past half-year, I had created significant goodwill equity with the Chief of Staff at the US Embassy. The AEP had missionaries throughout Albania, and all of these missionaries were connected by a radio network set up by Mission Aviation Fellowship and semi-managed by the AEP. Whenever there was unrest in the country, which these days was often, I was a pipeline of information to the US Embassy. I had yet to cash in my favor chips for all of my efforts on their behalf. It now became apparent that today would be the day for a payout.

With the radio we had in the van, I was able to message Michelle and ask her to immediately call the Embassy's Chief of Staff in Tirana. I asked her to use my name, explain our situation, and tell them what had just transpired. Michelle got to work. We sat and waited for a miracle, which was all we could do at this point. Within twenty minutes, we could see the dust on the horizon approaching the airport. It was the US Embassy convoy returning. Michelle's call had worked, and the attitude and demeanor of the head of security had taken a one-eighty-degree turn. We were now a treasure to be guarded at all costs and would be escorted all the way to our home in Tirana.

With multiple embassy vehicles in front and behind, we set off for the capital. Armed embassy personnel were hanging out of every available vehicular window to remind any would-be evildoer that they meant business. And so, we zoomed down the highway headed toward Tirana. Nani was now smiling from ear to ear and in his element. I could tell that in his wildest dreams, he could not have imagined a scenario like this unfolding. As we made our way into the city, the roadways were completely void of people and traffic. Everyone had locked themselves indoors for the evening with the hope that tomorrow would bring some form of normalcy to the city streets.

As our convoy pulled up to our house, our neighbors from the many high-rise apartment buildings surrounding us peeked out their windows to see what was happening. Immediately upon stopping, all of the security personnel exited their SUVs with rifles creating a safety corridor that allowed us to walk across the street and into our front door. Many of our neighbors had wondered what had brought the Mann family to Albania, and from that moment forward, we would never convince them that we were not employees of the CIA.

We made it. We were home. Mom was thrilled to see the kids. The kids, oblivious to everything taking place, were all so happy to see Oma. As Mom hugged and greeted Michelle, her first comment was, "That ride into town was fine. I don't see what all of this fuss is about."

Unfortunately, the day's excitement was not over. I still had the CNN reporter with us. He needed to get to his hotel in the center of downtown, which was several blocks from our house. Not wanting to be outside after dark, I set off with him for the Hotel Tirana, the same hotel where Michelle and I had stayed on our very first visit to Albania. We walked quickly but cautiously, stopping at street corners and doing our best to avoid venturing into exposed areas. In short order, I had delivered him downtown. He thanked me for the help I had provided. If he had truly understood the circumstances of the day, ours would have been the lead story on CNN the next morning.

My journey home was a bit more exciting. I was caught in crossfire at least twice, and after spending a decent amount of time prostrate on the ground, I eventually made it home as darkness descended on Tirana. With the failure of the attempted coup, life returned to normal in Albania the next day.

With the approach of fall, 1998, the Kosovo refugee influx into Albania continued unabated. The AEP Crisis Center had now opened several locations for refugees around the country. One was in Tirana, and another was in the northern Albanian city of Bajram Curri, which was in close proximity to the border with Kosovo. Both of these projects were funded through substantial grants by the United Nations High Commissioner for Refugees (UNHCR). It was incumbent on me to monitor the Bajram Curri site as it was being prepared to receive refugees in the north.

I left our home early one beautiful fall morning and arrived at our facility in Bajram Curri mid-afternoon. After a few hours at the center, a social worker who had been assigned to our northern team asked me if I would like to pay a domestic visit to a local home that was housing a refugee family. Wanting to inspect all aspects of what I was overseeing, I readily agreed. Two social workers, a driver, and I headed across town.

Erik Stensland and his wife, Joanna, were the missionaries we had stayed with when we first arrived in Albania. Erik was working with the Evangelical Alliance in Albania, and Joanna was my office manager at the AEP. Erik and Joanna had both lived in Bajram Curri, one of the most difficult regions of Albania. Because of this, they had my immense respect.

Erik was the mastermind behind finding the AEP drivers in this lawless region. Bajram Curri, and most of the surrounding area for that matter, was controlled by clan families. Nothing of importance took place without clan approval. Erik, in his wisdom, enlisted the assistance of the largest clan in Bajram Curri in providing us drivers for our AEP/United Nations SUVs. His rationale was simple: everyone in town would know that the largest and most powerful clan had the "contract" for driving the AEP/UN vehicles. Therefore, everyone would be too scared of clan retaliation to interfere with AEP/UN activities. This made perfect sense to me. I was grateful that Erik had been able to make these arrangements, thanks to the good relationships he had made during his time living in the area.

Our visit with the refugee family lasted less than an hour. Now the sun was beginning to set. We returned to our conspicuously new UN Toyota Landcruiser and set off to return to the refugee center. Not five minutes into our drive, we turned left onto a dirt roadway. A few seconds further, we noticed a small, red sedan heading straight toward us. It was obvious that this vehicle was attempting to block our way. Our driver slowed to a stop as the small red car screeched to a halt directly in front of us. Clearly visible in the passenger seat of the red car was a man pointing an AK-47 our direction.

As this armed gunman exited his vehicle, two things happened simultaneously. First, our driver threw the car into reverse and immediately began to reverse course. Not wanting to die this day, all the passengers screamed to our driver in nearly synchronized harmony, "STOP!" Our request proved unnecessary, as this was the moment that the second event occurred. A second vehicle slid behind us to block our escape. Our driver was pinned in and now forced to halt.

Now, multiple AK-47s were leveled at us, both from in front and from behind our vehicle. The man who had exited the passenger side of the red sedan was now opening our driver's door. The assailant gave our driver a brotherly slap on the cheek as he forced him to exit the car. This was a curious event as the slap was less a violent act and more like the winning move in a friendly chess match. With others pointing guns at us, we were ordered to leave everything in the car and get out. We got out as quickly as possible. With armed men assuming our places in the Toyota, doors slammed, and all three vehicles sped off in a matter of seconds. The four of us were left standing in a cloud of dust on the side of the road at the edge of town. My sole act of defiance toward these bandits was that I retained possession of the camera I had been ordered to leave in the car.

After a few moments of standing silently together in a state of shock, we made the long, slow hike back into town. That evening over dinner, several of us discussed the events of the afternoon. That discussion made me forever leery of eyewitness testimony. I remembered the car being red. Another remembered the car as blue. I remembered three gunmen; another remembered four – and on and on. At the end of dinner, all that we could agree on was the fact that we had been carjacked. It was later discovered that a rival clan had, indeed, orchestrated the event. Since the carjackers did not want to start a clan war, they had attempted to be kind to our driver. Our vehicle was never recovered.

A month after this incident, a letter arrived from a donor in Pittsburgh. He had received a newsletter I had written to our supporters in which I described my carjacking in Bajram Curri. His note was in response to my correspondence. He informed me that on the day of my carjacking, unaware of my circumstances and half a world away; he had been prompted by the Lord to pull his car over to the side of the road and pray for me. Taking into consideration the time difference, he had been led to pray for me on the exact day and at the exact time I was being carjacked.

As the autumn leaves in Albania began to fall, AEP's annual meeting in Corfu, Greece, was also upon us. This year's meeting would be especially problematic because of the security issues in regard to traveling the country's roadways. Typically, the AEP would fill a bus with members and their families and drive from Tirana to the coastal city of Sarande. From there, the group would take a short ferry ride over to the isle of Corfu. Unfortunately, the only direct route to Sarande would take us through the lawless town of Lazarat, which was controlled by clans and ungovernable gangs.

This year, in light of our security concerns, the AEP leadership decided this trip could only be safely made if we were to organize a police escort for the bus as it traveled through Lazarat. Some were skeptical that this would be enough, as the Albanian police force had been known to run rather than fight in the event of a conflict. But as this was one of our only options, we began to make arrangements with the proper authorities for this security escort.

On the day of our trip, things went well. When we arrived at the outskirts of Lazarat, loaded with a full contingency of missionary families, the Albanian police were there to meet us with a motorcycle escort. We were ushered through the next several miles of troubled roadway by our misfit guardians and then sent on our way to Sarande. We arrived in Corfu several hours later, the journey having gone according to plan.

After a delightful few days of meetings mixed with relaxation, it was time to make our return journey back to Tirana. With things having gone so well getting to Corfu, everyone was optimistic that our drive home would be equally uneventful. And our trip was uneventful until we arrived at the outskirts of Lazarat. No police presence was waiting for us, despite our confirmation with the police station that they would be on scene. Now a decision had to be made. Do we venture on without a police escort, or do we sit on the outskirts of Lazarat for an extended period of time with a full bus of missionary families waiting for the police to arrive? Either option could have dangerous consequences. After a prolonged wait as we deliberated the issue, the decision was made by our leadership team that we would forge ahead without our police escort. It would be twenty minutes of uncertainty before we would be out of danger and homeward bound.

So we started again, still confident that all would be well. That confidence lasted only until our bus broke down in the middle of Lazarat's danger zone. Now we had a real problem. Unknown to us at the time, a couple of fast-thinking Albanian entrepreneurs and owners of their own bus had spotted us miles before as we experienced mechanical issues. They had decided to follow our bus to see if their services might be required. As we broke down on the side of the Lazarat roadway, these businessmen and their bus pulled in front of us.

Now the debate with my team resumed while a decision as to what to do next needed to be made quickly. Some, seeing a miracle in the making, thought that the second bus had been providentially provided for our safe passage. Others rightly pointed out that it was very suspicious that this bus had been following us. How could these two gentlemen have known that we were having mechanical problems? Maybe it was a strangely orchestrated trap. No one knew these men. What if, in fact, they were not the good guys but the bad guys? This discussion became quite heated and carried on much longer than was reasonable. Every moment we spent arguing about what to do next put us in greater danger.

The time for debate had expired. A decision was required. Joshua and Caleb were the only two spies who had been sent by Israel to scout out Canaan, who returned with a good report. The other ten spies were overwhelmed with doubt and fear in regard to what lay before them. I saw the circumstances we were experiencing as our Joshua moment. This second bus was indeed providential, a gift from the Lord for our safe deliverance. That was my decision.

We quickly negotiated a fee for the services of our new drivers, and we immediately loaded the families onto the new bus. The new bus was smaller than the one we had been using, and it could not accommodate our luggage. Even had there been adequate room for our baggage, the process involved to transfer the luggage to the new bus would have taken far too long. It was decided that as soon as everyone boarded the bus, we would depart without our belongings. Hopefully, our old bus could be quickly repaired by our driver and join us soon with our possessions. That's exactly what transpired. Within a brief period of time following our safe arrival in Tirana, we were reunited with our old bus and our personal property. Our trip to Corfu had become memorable after all.

Our team at the AEP worked hard through difficult circumstances during 1998. The war in Kosovo had seen to it that we were continuously busy. When we weren't meeting the needs of AEP members, we were helping refugees. Because of this, I felt our team deserved some time away from the busyness of Albania. Mike Jeffries came to my aid once again. First Baptist Church Ft. Lauderdale agreed to fly our AEP staff to Germany for a short R&R break. Bob and Hanne Wittenzellner, as well as other friends from our time in Bavaria, opened their homes to our small group. Our trip took place near the first Advent. We enjoyed celebrating some of Germany's beautiful Christmas traditions. This trip was a welcome respite from Tirana's dirt and dust.

Step by step, in my role as AEP Administrator, I was learning to be a better servant leader. Managing a much larger team that was comprised of different nationalities forced me to deal with new problems. In addition to work issues, staff members came to me with their personal troubles. I also had many in the expatriate missionary community in Albania come to me for advice. I was doing my best to quickly learn how to be a leader, and I found that my previous fears of having to "earn my place at the table" were no longer relevant. There wasn't a lot of time for self-reflection in regard to my leadership style. I recognized that a critical job needed to be done in Albania. I had been the one assigned to do it, so I needed to get to work.

I was also learning that being young and under-experienced had nothing to do with leadership. Being a servant was the real qualifier. In Luke 22: 19–20, Jesus said to His disciples, "The greatest among you should be like the youngest, and the one who rules like the one who serves. For who is greater, the one who is at the table or the one who serves? Is it not the one who is at the table? But I am among you as the one who serves" (Luke 22:19–20, NIV).

With the arrival of 1999, the fear of Y2K was in full swing around the world. Y2K, or the Millennium Bug, as many referred to it, was the fear that technology had not made allowances for software date formatting to transition into the new millennium. Panic as to what would happen to the world's computers on January 1st, 2000, was everywhere. The fear was that at the stroke of midnight on the turn of the millennium, computer operating systems around the world would fail. Everything from power stations to banks, airlines to personal computers – it was all at risk. While most sectors of industry had uncovered the problem years earlier and had been working on their own "fixes" to solve the issue, there was an ever-growing concern that on midnight of December 31st, 1999, the world would return to the dark ages.

For Albanians, in a country that never had a stable power supply, there was no such anxiety. More relevant to us was the continuing war in Kosovo and the refugee crisis that only worsened. By this time, Evangelical churches across Albania were taking care of a large percentage of the refugees flooding into this Balkan nation. The AEP continued to do its part to help. Refugee centers both in the north of the country and in Tirana were still operating. The AEP also supported local Albanian churches and in-country mission organizations in their efforts to care for the Kosovo refugees. When opportunities arose for the AEP to engage in some new type of outreach to the refugees, it often accepted the challenge.

One such campaign took place on Easter at the northern Albanian border with Kosovo near the city of Kükes. Kosovar refugees had been pouring over that border for some time, with Kükes being the first city they reached upon arrival in Albania. Many Americans remember the images on the TV news of mile after mile of Kosovars driving their tractors across the border and towing behind them their family and all their remaining earthly possessions. As this situation worsened, the AEP and the Albanian Evangelical Alliance decided to create welcome teams that would meet these Kosovars at the border and help facilitate their transition from war victim to refugee. We prayed that Christians welcoming these Muslim believers with open arms would have a lasting positive impact.

Our team traveled to Kükes very early on the Saturday morning before Easter. The trip was both long and nauseating. The winding roads and cramped conditions in the van made more than one traveler lose their breakfast or lunch somewhere along the journey. We arrived in Kükes mid-afternoon to a surreal sight. In the central portion of downtown, many of the refugees had gathered for what was going to be a distribution of food by the Albanian government. On one side of the street, the world's media had gathered to record this event as it unfolded. Their television vans were parked next to each other in a long row that stretched down the entire side of the boulevard. Their satellite antennas were pointed toward the sky, ready to live-stream the misfortunes of these refugees. I recognized the world-famous CNN reporter Christiana Amanpour among the group of reporters.

As I watched from a different vantage point, I noticed that the distribution of aid was about to begin. With shock, I looked on as dump trucks rolled into the town plaza that was filled with refugees. The dump trucks were loaded with loaves of bread, and they began to slowly drive through the middle of the crowd. When the refugees realized what was happening, they charged forward toward the back of the trucks. Men, perched high enough in the trucks to avoid the refugee onslaught, launched loaves of bread out the back, down onto the men and women who were now fighting for the loaves raining down on them. Watching humans fight each other for food was a woeful sight. All the while, CNN was broadcasting this event live into the well-stocked kitchens and dining rooms of America.

As the trucks finished their distribution and drove off into the distance, the crowd slowly began to disperse. It appeared that there had been no serious injuries during this "distribution of aid," which in and of itself was a miracle.

My team and I now headed to a local church that was the basecamp for our refugee operations. For some time, we had organized teams that would take trips to the border where the refugees were crossing into Albania. These teams would bring with them food, water, and medical aid to distribute among the refugees who were waiting to cross into Albania in the long line of tractors and trailers. Often the aid that our staff provided was the first assistance these refugees had received after many days of travel. Most told unbelievable stories of barely escaping their homes as the Serbian army attacked. Many stories told were of seeing family members raped, tortured, and murdered. Desperation and heartbreak were elements that every account had in common.

As darkness began to fall on Kükes, our team would bed down overnight in the church. A second team would then take over the job of welcoming arriving refugees throughout the evening. The flow of refugees never stopped. We had to make ourselves available twenty-four hours of the day. As our day came to a close, those of us off-duty spread our sleeping bags on the church floor and tried to rest. The church was always busy with team members coming and going. Pure exhaustion from the day's events was the only reason I was able to fall asleep.

Early Easter morning, 1999, I was awakened by a commotion in the church building. Sometime during the course of the last few hours, one of our welcome teams had discovered a problem among one of the refugee families fleeing Kosovo. A young mother, who was transported in a wagon pulled by her family's tractor, was on the verge of death. The family had escaped their home with just their lives as the Serbs moved in to destroy their every possession.

Even though they had escaped, this young mother was not out of danger. Due to her failing kidneys, she required dialysis several times a week to live. This family had been fleeing for over a week, and the elderly parents had no chance of getting their daughter help. Fortunately, one of our team members from the UK, Steven Kemp, was a nurse. Steven immediately made his way to the convoy of tractors, where this family was located to assess the situation.

When Steven returned, he had bad news. If this woman did not receive urgent medical treatment, she would die. The entire country of Albania had only a few dialysis machines, and they were all at a single hospital in Tirana. Communication began with the UN representatives in Kükes to see if there was anything that could be done. We were told that our best chance of getting this young woman help was to wait on a UN helicopter that had been called for an emergency medical evacuation. This was great news. The bad news was that the ETA for this helicopter was still several hours from now. There was serious doubt that this young woman would be able to survive that long.

As we debated if anything else could be done, an Albanian military helicopter landed at our site. When the call for an emergency medical evacuation had gone out, the UN had also called the Albanian government, which for once was able to respond quickly. The helicopter had arrived to transport our patient to Tirana. Looking at this helicopter, it appeared to be decades old, and it was most certainly made in China. It was a death machine. Whoever stepped into this whirlybird had a fifty-fifty chance of surviving the experience. But we had no other choice.

It was decided that both Steven and I would accompany the young woman and her elderly father on the flight to Tirana. Steven was needed because he had the medical expertise if anything went wrong on the airlift. He would also be able to inform those receiving us in Tirana of the young woman's medical needs. I went along because, as the leader of the team, I had some authority to make things happen. I had the potential to be helpful if we ran into any administrative roadblocks along our way.

We boarded the aircraft and attempted to make our young charge comfortable. We wrapped her in my down sleeping bag, which seemed to comfort her, and we lifted off. I have done many scary things in my lifetime, and flying in this tin can is at the top of my most petrifying list. The noises that the helicopter made were both deafening and terrifying. Our flight was just over thirty minutes, but it seemed an eternity.

When we landed at the military hospital in Tirana, an ambulance was waiting to take the young woman and her father to the Tirana hospital with the dialysis machines. Throughout the week, our AEP office made sure that she received the needed medical treatments. In a week's time, we were able to help coordinate her transfer to facilities in Italy, which were far superior to Albania's hospitals.

Easter Sunday, 1999, was a memorable experience. I have always been grateful that as the world celebrated the resurrection and new life of our Lord and Savior Jesus Christ, I was allowed to play a small role in saving a life. I often wonder what became of that young Kosovar mother.

By June, the war in Kosovo had ended. We witnessed one of the fastest repatriations of refugees returning to their homeland in modern history. Within a period of a few short months, the majority of refugees in Albania were back in Kosovo. It was unimaginable that the small evangelical community in Albania had taken care of the majority of refugees who had entered the country. For years, people around the world had prayed that the Muslims of Kosovo would be open to the Gospel of Jesus Christ. Now, refugees were returning to their homeland and were inviting the Christians, who had so admirably taken care of them while in exile, to be their honored guests. And thus, began the influx of Christian missionaries into Kosovo—the perfect example of something good coming out of a very difficult situation.

As refugees left Albania, it was time for the Mann family to leave as well. The two-year contract Michelle and I had signed with AEP was expiring. We began to make plans to return to the States, moving to the Chicago area where missionary friends were living. We hoped to collaborate with them in international mission work in the short-term as we continued to contemplate our prospects for the future.

An attorney from Chicago, Bob Baker, and his wife, Dalia, were selected by the AEP board of directors to succeed me in my position as AEP Administrator. I did not envy Bob, as he would be required to oversee the audit process of all we had undertaken the previous year during the refugee crisis. But I could not think of a more capable man to do the job. Our transition plan was for me to help the family return to the States in late summer, and then after a few weeks of assisting them to settle into a new home, I would return to Albania for a final month in order to help Bob in the AEP transition process.

According to schedule, in late summer, we said our goodbyes to the Land of the Eagles. Michelle and the kids were barely settled into our new environment in the Chicago suburbs when it was time for me to return to Albania for the final AEP handover. That month was long, but soon our small family was reunited in Crystal Lake, Illinois, ready to start the next, unknown chapter of what God had in store for us.

CHAPTER SEVEN
THE WALLS CAME TUMBLING DOWN

"It was by faith that the people of Israel marched around Jericho for seven days, and the walls came crashing down" (Hebrews 11:30, NLT).

It was by faith that Michelle and I returned to the United States, not fully understanding all that the Lord had next for us. We believed the walls of fear and uncertainty would fall if we continued to be open to hearing God's still, small voice in our lives. While we returned to the US with confidence God had great and unknown things ahead, we would soon find out the metaphor of walls crashing down would be applicable in other ways as well.

As our feet landed on US terra firma in late summer of 1999, our initial plan was to work with friends in the Chicago area who were involved in missionary efforts worldwide. One major blessing was while missionaries in Albania, we had been supported by a church in Crystal Lake, a suburb of Chicago. We planned to rent a home in the area, making the search for a place to worship much easier.

Michelle had two requests as we began to look for a home in the Chicago suburbs. First, a bathtub. Our house in Albania had a very small shower that was especially problematic when it came to bathing the kids and the dog. Second, she wanted a place where Andrew and Abby would be able to ride their bikes and trikes. The urban landscape of Tirana had not given our youngsters an opportunity to enjoy this favorite childhood pastime. While these requests were simple, finding affordable housing in the northwest suburbs of Chicago at the time proved difficult.

With the help of new church friends who understood the area's real estate market, God orchestrated a beautiful two-story home on the outskirts of Crystal Lake. Touring the house, we were certain the rental price would far exceed our budget. We had previously seen homes similar to this that were well beyond our financial reach. Michelle chatted with the owner, sharing with her our missionary experiences in Albania. As it turned out, our future landlord was also a Christian, and she offered the house to us on the spot at an unbelievably low monthly rental price.

As with the sale of our home in Texas, I was tone deaf to what was happening around me. I told the owner that we would think about it, and once again, Michelle gave me the "you must be insane" look. It was obvious that the Lord had opened this door of provision for our family – so we immediately accepted. The owner's one stipulation was that we did not get our hopes up in regard to purchasing the house, as her husband would never agree to sell it. We were ecstatic, to say the least. In addition to a long driveway and quiet streets to ride bikes, the house had three bathtubs!

Settling into life in America, we were confronted with a few initial surprises. With the help of Michelle's sister, Andrea, we located a Christian school for the kids near Crystal Lake—Trinity Oaks Christian Academy. Andrew was starting first grade, and Abby would be in pre-kindergarten. The children at Trinity Oaks had learned to read in kindergarten, so naturally, they entered first grade as readers. We were surprised to learn that Andrew had spent much of his kindergarten experience at the Albanian international school playing games and eating ice cream. His reading ability was well-behind that of his American peers.

Apparently, because of the diverse cultural backgrounds of the children at the Albanian international school, many of the younger children had great difficulty with the English language. Therefore, the educational experience that we had anticipated for Andrew had not taken place—discovering these details after the fact taught us the valuable lesson of staying engaged with our children's education. But learning that lesson was no consolation at the moment, as Andrew was now well-behind his classmates in reading.

Andrew suffered more than the rest of the family in regard to his reintegration to life in the USA. The low-key boy never complained though, as he was shuffled each day directly from school to his reading tutor and then to sports activities. In hindsight, being one of the younger first graders in his class, we should have allowed him to repeat kindergarten at Trinity Oaks. That wisdom, however, was not in the owner's manual for new parents. Without a manual, it is the firstborn who always suffers. In relatively short order, Andrew did catch up to his peers, but I continue to have feelings of guilt when I think about what Andrew went through that first year returning to America.

In December of 1999, public anxiety grew, and concern built over the fear that the Y2K millennium bug was about to bite hard. People stockpiled food and water, and a general feeling of unease was present with most of our friends and acquaintances. The Manns, having essentially lived Y2K in Albania for the previous two years with constant power and water outages, were not worried about the prospects of going without electricity for a few days or weeks. As everyone anxiously awaited the turn of a new millennium, December 31st, Michelle and I were almost disappointed when life went on as usual at the stroke of midnight.

That new year we continued to settle into our surroundings in Crystal Lake. We enjoyed making new friends through church and the Trinity Oaks school, and Andrew and Abby acclimated quickly to life as normal American kids. Michelle and I worked as self-employed, independent contractors with local friends who were engaged in mission activities worldwide. Michelle used her accounting skills as a CPA to help indigenous nationals in majority world countries, while I used the administrative talents I learned in Albania to have an impact on those we were serving internationally.

All the while, a passion for empowering Christian men and women globally in business was stirring in the core of my being. While living in Albania, I noticed Albanian nationals, who had a passion for evangelizing their own nation, struggling for the financial capacity to carry out their calling. So often, I witnessed them compromise what God had asked them to accomplish in their own country in exchange for financial security from the West. It was all too common that an American nonprofit organization or missionary would appear, offering a job and a salary – but with strings attached. Usually, these "strings" involved adapting to the vision dictated by the new paymaster.

Witnessing this scenario play out over and over again, I started to think there might be a better way of helping national believers carry out their God-given calling in life. What if we trained them in business, teaching them to create wealth? This would not only allow them to financially support their families, but it would simultaneously fund their mission endeavors. In 1999, when this concept was rattling through my head, few organizations, if any, had begun to think this far outside of the traditional mission box.

I began to research groups and organizations that were engaged in this type of forward-thinking empowerment. To my amazement, among my circles of contacts, this was a new concept in missions. When I inquired, none of my connections were interested in talking with me, much less hiring me to start such a new program for their organizations.

Michelle and I kept working and dreaming. We weren't the least bit discouraged, as we were seeing God use us in new ways since our return to the US. One new change was that Michelle and I were both doing independent international travel. In the past, I had done most of the traveling. With the children a bit older, Michelle was now busy as well, using her talents worldwide.

That April, through contacts in Albania, I made my first trip to Africa. I traveled to South Sudan to visit Leif Zetterlund and his organization, International Aid Services (IAS). IAS was a Swedish organization that specialized in WASH projects (water, sanitation, and hygiene) in East Africa. I traveled with Leif to consult on a business empowerment project they had begun in a rural area of South Sudan near Yei, just across the northern Ugandan border. The trip was an eye-opener, and it was my first exposure to a war-torn African nation. In fact, South Sudan villages were continuing to come under bombardment from Khartoum, Sudan, in the north. While I'm not confident my consultation was of great help to Leif, he and I connected on a personal level. This trip launched the beginning of decades of cooperative efforts between the two of us.

Not only was the trip to South Sudan enlightening, it was also frustrating. At that point in our lives, Michelle and I were scraping by financially. Because of this, I had traveled to South Sudan without any financial resources to leave behind. The immense amount of need I witnessed in South Sudan made me ashamed that I was not able to immediately provide more assistance. I was so frustrated by this experience that I pledged that I would never return to South Sudan without the resources necessary to make a social impact.

In November of 2000, Michelle made a trip to Shillong, India, to conduct a financial and leadership workshop for a contact in the region. Kitbok Ryntathiang, who ran both a Christian School in Shillong and an expansive ministry, was Michelle's host. During the course of Michelle's stay in Shillong, Kitbok gave Michelle a guided tour of the organization's other mission projects.

Our custom as a family was to sit together when one of us returned from a trip and view the traveler's photos from the journey. He or she got a chance to explain what they had seen and done while away. This was one technique Michelle and I used to keep Andrew and Abby engaged in our mission work. Michelle shared with us photos she had taken on the tour of Kitbok's orphanage. There were lots of pictures of the facilities and all of the beautiful children. However, one little girl, who appeared to be the youngest, stood out from all the others.

I could not get this little girl out of my mind even days after Michelle's return. In our line of work, we were continually confronted with children in difficult situations, and our hearts always went out to them. So why was I fixated on this little girl? What made this situation different? I was perplexed as to these feelings I was experiencing. After a week of keeping these thoughts to myself, I approached Michelle to discuss my mental conundrum. Michelle challenged me to begin praying as to why God was bringing this child to the forefront at this moment.

I prayed, and I was scared of what I believed the Lord was telling me. I was sensing in my spirit that Michelle and I were to adopt this little one named Elisheba, which translates to Elizabeth from Hebrew. Michelle and I had not discussed adoption in our ten years of marriage. Besides not knowing Michelle's feelings on adoption in general, I wasn't sure of my own feelings in this regard. So, partially hoping that Michelle would tell me I was crazy so that I could forget about the idea entirely, I went to her with how I felt the Lord was prompting me. And Michelle's response was simply, "Let me pray about it."

A few days later, now approaching the Christmas season, Michelle told me that she was confirming the same prompting of the Lord and that we should pass this idea along to Kitbok in India. In Kitbok's orphanage in Shillong, many of the children were not true orphans. This meant that many mothers and fathers had not given up their parental rights to their children. It was quite possible that Elisheba, or Elly as we began to call her, was in this category. Were this the situation, the entire discussion would come to a quick conclusion.

When we inquired with Kitbok about Elisheba, we discovered that not only was Elly an orphan, but Kitbok had been specifically praying for her. His prayer had been that God would use her in a mighty way in the future. To say that Kitbok was thrilled with our news was an understatement. And so began one of the hardest efforts of my life. It was a journey that would take over three years to complete.

As I began to make initial inquiries regarding how a self-organized international adoption might work, Christmas 2000 arrived. Our family traveled to Jacksonville, Florida, for the holiday season to be with Michelle's sister, Andrea, and her family. During the course of what was otherwise a delightful vacation, Michelle noticed a small lump in her breast. While not too concerned, it was disturbing enough for her to make a mental note to get it checked when she returned home.

Once we returned home, I was beginning to understand that an international adoption was not going to be an easy undertaking. Before we started this process, I had no understanding of the procedures required for an international adoption. Most, if not all, international adoption agencies have developed relationships with patterning agencies abroad. A network of adoptable children is in place between these sister organizations, and adoptions are arranged based on the children in these networks. I could not find one adoption agency that would let a couple choose their own child for adoption in a foreign country. This meant that we would be required to organize this ourselves.

We also discovered that, according to Indian adoption law, all international adoptions must take place through both US and Indian agencies that have a working relationship with an Indian adoption clearinghouse known as the Central Adoption Resource Authority, or CARA. Practically speaking, this meant that we would be required to find an adoption agency in the US that was recognized by CARA to handle our paperwork. Then, an additional agency in India must be selected, that was also recognized by CARA to facilitate the international side of the adoption.

What I discovered through friends who had successfully navigated an international adoption was the Tulsa, Oklahoma based agency, Dillon International. Dillon was recognized by CARA, and they agreed to function as the US clearinghouse for the legal aspects of our adoption, on the condition that I would organize things internationally. Of course, I had no idea how to go about organizing an international adoption, but this relationship with Dillon seemed like a great start to this monumental enterprise.

In a move that, in hindsight, proved unwise, Kitbok informed Elly early in the process of our plans to adopt. By sharing this news with Elly, we had given a four-year-old an undue burden to carry for a long period of time, especially considering that success was not guaranteed. Unimaginable at the time, Elly's adoption would eventually take over three years to complete. We also involved our kids in the adoption process early in the journey, but for different reasons. Elly would be joining our family, and much like having a baby, we wanted Andrew and Abby to be a part of this adventure as well. As the days moved forward, both of the children embraced the idea of having a sister from India.

When I began to get the adoption process started in India, I discovered that Elly had no official documentation proving she was an orphan. Even worse, she did not have a birth certificate. Before any further steps could be taken, these documents had to be created by local governmental agencies. As we would discover, while Elly was an orphan, she did have living relatives who loved her. These relatives had to be contacted and asked if they were in agreement with Elly being adopted internationally. Although they could not take care of Elly physically, it was hard for them to imagine Elly leaving the country for a new life in the United States. Elly's extended family were Christians, and they ultimately came to the determination that Elly living with our family in America was the Lord's will and the best chance for her to have limitless opportunities.

As the process of getting Elly's personal documentation in order wore on, Michelle had been given a referral by her local doctor in Illinois to a breast cancer specialist in Madison, Wisconsin, not far from our home. After a routine exam by the physician in February of 2001, Michelle was assured that she should not worry. Michelle was told by Dr. Mack that it was common for women of her age to have fibroadenomas. Doctor Mack told her that her lump would grow, but not to be concerned. We left the doctor's office reassured that we could now stop thinking about the small lump.

With so much going on in our lives, Michelle and I were also making some major career decisions. Desiring to work with majority world empowerment programs through business development, but not finding any organizations that shared my passion, Michelle and I decided to start our own nonprofit organization – Global Business Assist (GBA). We were busy that spring and summer establishing the legal structure for the organization, filing for nonprofit status with the IRS, and selecting a board of directors. Finding donors for the new organization was necessary as well. We even took an initial team of business teachers into South Sudan in March, which was very successful. The challenges of building GBA into a viable nonprofit were just beginning, but we were excited by the new ministry vision before us.

During the summer of 2001, our family took a short vacation to Ouray, Colorado, which is home for much of Michelle's side of the family. Although Dr. Mack in Wisconsin had told Michelle in February not to worry about her lump, putting it out of her mind was not that simple. Michelle voiced her continued concerns to me throughout that spring and summer, and I was not very supportive. I reminded her of Dr. Mack's pedigree as one of the leading names in his field at the University of Wisconsin. Surely, he knew his business, and if he was not troubled, why should we be concerned? My lack of support for Michelle and her feelings related to her health concerns remains one of my biggest life regrets. On vacation in the beautiful mountains of Colorado, as we discussed once again, Michelle's unease with her growing lump, we agreed that it should be biopsied once we returned home.

Michelle's biopsy was scheduled to take place in early October in Madison, Wisconsin, with Dr. Mack. When the day arrived for her exam, we approached this event with some foreboding. However, we were once again robustly reassured by the doctor that Michelle had nothing to fear. According to Dr. Mack, he would, of course, biopsy the lump, but it would only prove what he already knew—that it was a fibroadenoma. Following the exam, we drove home to Crystal Lake on that beautiful fall day feeling more at ease and looking forward to a pleasant weekend. On Sunday evening, we received the call that shook our world. At the age of thirty-five, Michelle had cancer.

This turn of events began a chapter in our lives that would continue in various ways for the better part of a decade. In an attempt to prepare our children for this health journey, Michelle and I took five-year-old Abby to lunch for a private conversation. As Michelle carefully and lovingly attempted to steady Abby for the fact that Mom would be losing her hair in this process, our sweet and loving daughter was unfazed by the news. Obviously, having heard too many commercials on Christian radio, her response was simply, "It's OK, Mom. You can just use Rogaine!"

Months later, Michelle was preparing to tuck Abby into bed one evening. In a quiet and intimate moment between mom and daughter, Abby reached up and rubbed Michelle's now hairless head. Abby said to her, "Mom, I really like your bald head!" Andrew and Abby were truly a blessing throughout this family trial.

While Michelle's battle with cancer is also interwoven in my life's journey, it is her story to tell. The strength that I witnessed from my wife as she walked through fire was unparalleled. With young children to raise, she never let the struggle that was ahead diminish her love and care for her family. Through the hardest of times, she remained a rock, and she powered through every challenge and overcame every adversity. Of all the things I may hope to accomplish in this lifetime, not one of them will equal the strength and courage Michelle exemplified to her family through her confrontation with cancer. While I do not dare tell her story, I will celebrate with Michelle her victory.

Another Christmas season came and went, and 2002 was ushered in with more adoption challenges. Kitbok was having difficulty compiling Elly's official documentation, and Michelle's cancer diagnosis had created a new problem. Even though I was managing the international side of the adoption, Dillon informed us that Michelle's cancer was an automatic adoption disqualification for at least five to ten years as per Dillon's guidelines. We were heartbroken. In the midst of this sorrow, I remember one Sunday morning, God speaking sweetly and softly to my spirit, reminding me that He was in charge of this process.

In a still, small voice, I felt the Lord say to me, "Who told you that you couldn't adopt?" My immediate, internal reply was, "Well, the Dillon Agency." I then heard coming from the same quiet voice, "Don't stop until I have closed the door." After such encouragement, I began to inquire with Dillon if there were possible exceptions to the rules pertaining to cancer.

I discussed with Tami, our Dillon representative, what options might still be available. I was told that a direct appeal to the Dillon board of directors was the only way this barrier could be overcome. I put together a case as to why the board should grant our request to move forward with the adoption, including a letter from Michelle's physician that cited a good long-term prognosis for Michelle. We submitted these documents and then waited for the day that the board would meet to discuss our adoption. I was so nervous on the day we expected the final decision from the board that I didn't want to answer the telephone. But all of my worry was for naught, as God had once again cleared another hurdle for our family. The Dillon International board agreed to allow Michelle and me to continue pursuing our adoption of Elisheba.

Early in the development of GBA, I created a unified branding for the new organization. This was to include similar themes throughout all of our publications, including our website. This involved new design images and printed materials, and it was a big undertaking. To this end, I hired a graphic designer recommended by Mike Jeffries. We signed a contract for this project, and the graphic artist got to work on all the design elements required. Several months later, when everything was completed, I was pleased with the outcome. It was obvious that the graphic designer had underbid the job and had worked many hours on the task beyond what he had anticipated. Nevertheless, I congratulated myself on getting a good deal and vowed to continue to use this designer's excellent services in the future.

A few weeks after the completion of this project, I received the graphic designer's bill. The amount GBA was charged was substantially greater than the sum in our signed contract. My immediate inclination was to write a check for our agreed upon total and reference our signed contract. However, before I could do this, the Holy Spirit stopped me. I knew that this gentleman had done an excellent job and had worked overtime on my project. He had simply

underbid his services. Realizing these facts, I felt prompted
to pay him the full amount I was billed. The problem was
that we didn't have the money. This was a much larger sum
than I had anticipated, and, as a fledgling organization, GBA
did not have the funds. Additionally, I knew that Michelle,
as a CPA tracking our organizational finances, would not
be happy. I would be telling her that I was about to pay a
bill we didn't legally owe with money we didn't have in our
bank account.

But, the longer I pondered this predicament, the more
convinced I was that I needed to pay this invoice, even if
it caused us financial problems. I told Michelle what I was
doing, and as predicted, she was none too pleased. I put
the check in an envelope and departed for the post office. It
was difficult to mail that letter. I knew that if the check was
quickly cashed, we would potentially overdraw our newly
opened corporate bank account. I mailed the check anyway
and vowed that I would not dwell on the potential problems
this could create. If God was asking me to pay this bill, then
He would need to provide the financial resources necessary
to keep the check from bouncing higher than a rubber ball.

On my way home, I stopped at a second postal facility to
pick up our organizational mail from the previous day.
Inside the GBA postal box was a letter from a previously
unknown individual. Included with the letter was a check
to the organization that more than covered the invoice I had
paid just a few moments earlier. I was beginning to realize
in this new endeavor; if I listened to the Lord's direction
for our small organization, I could trust the Lord to be the
source of our provision. This would become a key refrain
as I taught business principles worldwide moving forward:

As Christians, "the God factor" becomes our competitive advantage!

With the arrival of spring in 2002, good news in Elly's adoption process arrived as well. Kitbok finally secured documentation that both proved Elly's birth and her status as an orphan. This was a significant development. But another hiccup had occurred over the winter months. Someone in Elly's small, rural village had objected to the international adoption. This put a temporary stop to everything. Kitbok began to investigate. He traveled to Elly's village many miles from the orphanage in Shillong to see if he could intervene.

In the meantime, we prayed. Michelle and I had agreed that we would keep Andrew and Abby informed as to every miracle and every challenge as we worked to bring Elly into our family. We knew that this involved all of us. The significance of the endeavor necessitated we share each joy and each sorrow along the way. Of course, our church and close friends were praying as well. This adoption was a community event.

When I talked with Kitbok one spring afternoon of 2002, he informed me that the person who had lodged the complaint with the state government concerning Elly's adoption had now withdrawn that objection. While we never understood the circumstances surrounding this change of heart, Michelle and I were convinced that Kitbok's intervention had played a crucial role. Regardless of how it happened, we saw the change in circumstances as yet another miracle and further confirmation that Elly would be joining the Manns. Things were beginning to look up!

Dillon International, our US adoption agency that was coordinating the legal side of the adoption once Elly arrived in the US, had a sister agency in Calcutta, India. It was The Indian Society for the Rehabilitation of Children. The state of Meghalaya, where Elly was currently located, had no international adoption agreements with the US. Because of this, Elly would need to be transferred from Kitbok's orphanage. The new orphanage would need to be located in another state of India, and it would need to be recognized by CARA in order to facilitate the final stage of the adoption process.

Dillon had communicated with its partner agency in Calcutta, and they agreed to receive Elly, as well as process the paperwork for the final phase of the adoption. We were told that this orphanage in Calcutta was a "babies only" orphanage, but they had nonetheless accepted Elly. With the transfer order for Elly in hand from the office of the Deputy Commissioner, East Khasi Hills District, Shillong, Meghalaya, our excitement grew by leaps and bounds.

That fall, we anxiously awaited the good news of Elly's safe transfer to Calcutta. Kitbok was to fly with Elly to Calcutta to organize the handover. However, the report we received a day after their scheduled flight was anything but good. Apparently, things had not gone well from the moment Kitbok met the new orphanage director, Mrs. Roy. Kitbok was not impressed with the orphanage leadership. Nor had he found the "babies only" facility a conducive environment for Elly. The feelings between Kitbok and Mrs. Roy must have been mutual, as the entire transfer to Calcutta was immediately called off. Kitbok and Elly returned to Shillong.

I was particularly perplexed by what had transpired. From my perspective, anything could be negotiated; anything could be worked out; anything could be tolerated for a period of time. Why were both sides adamant that this would not work? Didn't they understand that this might be our only option in regard to moving this adoption forward? I was convinced that the Dillon connection with the Calcutta orphanage was providential. It would be so simple to facilitate Elly's transfer working with a Dillon affiliate. Now it appeared that we were back to square one. My emotions were beginning to fray. I was finding all of these developments hard to understand.

While it never was clear what exactly occurred in Calcutta, one thing was certain – the Calcutta orphanage was no longer an option. As the curtain began to fall on 2002, Kitbok and I regrouped and developed an alternate approach. "Plan B" would involve finding an orphanage in New Delhi, the capital of India, for Elly's transfer.

After three years of living in Crystal Lake, our family was now firmly planted in the community. While we loved our rental house, we sensed that it might be time to buy a home in the area rather than continue leasing. Remembering what our landlord had said about her husband not wanting to sell the house, we did not inquire into this possibility. Rather, we began to look for other purchase options in our area and quickly determined that almost everything available to purchase was out of our price range.

After coming up empty in the hunt for a home, I reluctantly approached our landlords to ask if they might reconsider their stance on selling us the house. To our great surprise, the husband agreed to sell, for a reasonable price, and with no realtor fees involved. Once again, the hand of the Lord had orchestrated what before had been a closed door. On December 18, 2002, we signed the closing documents on our home on Garden Lane!

Global Business Assist was now growing. It was exciting starting new empowerment endeavors overseas. One of our first international projects was to assist an Albanian missionary couple, Juli and Enka Shtembari, in planting a church in Kosovo. Juli and Enka desired to start a language school in the town where they were living, Peje, to support themselves as church planters. They needed both capital and business expertise in order to get started. Juli and Enka were recipients of GBA's first empowerment grant – $10,000. They remain one of GBA's greatest success stories. In fact, Juli and Enka belong to a very elite club. They are among just a few of the businesses I've helped start that gave back financially to GBA once their venture prospered.

Teams from GBA were now traveling to the Balkans and Africa, and doors were opening for work in Asia as well. As we began to hone our training materials, which taught people how to start small enterprises, we developed a curriculum called "The Values Based Entrepreneur." This became a versatile tool as we expanded our reach internationally. GBA's relationship with Leif Zetterlund and International Aid Services was also expanding. In areas where IAS concentrated on drilling wells and completing sanitation projects, GBA became the defacto training arm for community business empowerment programs for IAS. The scope of IAS projects in Africa was so expansive that within just a few years, GBA was concentrating a majority of our efforts on assisting IAS throughout East Africa with our business expertise.

From a leadership perspective, I was now learning to run all aspects of an organization and to manage a predominantly volunteer staff. While working with a board of directors was not new to me, it was a bit different working with a board for an organization I had founded. As the one who cast the vision for our organizational efforts, I found it challenging to motivate board members to be equally as passionate about majority world business empowerment. Getting men and women with busy careers excited about the work of GBA wasn't always easy.

I was understanding for the first time the differences between an organization managed by paid employees and one that was run by volunteers. Learning how to motivate volunteers to undertake essential jobs was new to me. I realized that volunteers respond best to servant leaders who motivate, challenge, and lead through example. I discovered that volunteers do not respond positively to demanding and ungrateful leaders. I decided I did not want to become that type of manager.

In early 2003, Kitbok and I found an orphanage in New Delhi that could serve as a transfer point for Elly. It was The Ashran Hope Foundation and was directed by Mrs. Usha Franklin. This orphanage was licensed to complete international adoptions by CARA, and it had both babies and young children as residents. After further assessment, it was decided that this institution was our best option for completing the adoption. As quickly as possible, we began the paperwork required to facilitate Elly's transfer.

To assist with the final stage of the adoption process, I had now hired an attorney in New Delhi, Upamanyu Hazarika. This attorney would be our liaison between the Indian government and the local adoption agency in New Delhi. An unimaginable amount of paperwork was needed. I spent months signing documents, having the US government notarize them, and then having the Indian government do the same. For every document, there would be at least a two- or three-step process, each step often taking months to complete. My life became managing paperwork in some semi-state of completion, sent to one governmental office or another. My car could now navigate by itself to our local FedEx office.

If I thought my life was difficult, things were not easier for poor Elly. Elly was uprooted from the only home she had ever known, Kitbok's loving orphanage, and transported a thousand miles away. She was sent to a new part of India, with new faces, a new language to learn, and uncertainty about her future. All of these epic challenges confronted this little girl.

Elly's native language in her village of Hahim was Garo, also known as Achick. When Elly moved to the orphanage in Shillong, she learned Khasi, which is primarily spoken throughout that state of Meghalaya. In Kitbok's school at the orphanage, Elly learned English, which was the school's primary language. Now, on her arrival in New Delhi, Elly would be required to learn Hindi. It would be her fourth language before her sixth birthday.

The cost of Michelle's cancer treatment and the expense of an international adoption was proving to be a problem living on a missionary salary. Every new document and every additional hour the attorney worked on our behalf amounted to money we were finding hard to secure. To assist with our adoption expenses, two of our close friends,

Scott and Michelle Cufr, wrote a letter on our behalf
to friends and family from around the country asking
them to contribute to an adoption fund for Elly. Without
this assistance from so many who loved our family, we
would not have been able to bring Elly home. God used a
community to surround us with His love and provision.
Together with the funds we had saved and the money that
was donated on Elly's behalf, we had enough to finalize all
of our adoption expenses.

The year 2003 began to drag on like a two-run, fifteen-inning
baseball game. It seemed more documents for the adoption
were always needed. Just as things would start to look up, a
new wrinkle would develop. I had the feeling that we were
always moving two steps forward and one step backward.
The third year of this ordeal loomed bright in the headlights;
this challenge was never-ending.

The dog days of summer were upon us. Now, two new
adoption setbacks froze us in our tracks. The first stunning
development was the news that by Indian law, Elly would
be required to be offered for adoption to a local Indian
family. Should no Indian family request to adopt her, only
then would we have the chance to step forward. We were
stunned, and this disclosure quite frankly scared Michelle
and me to death. Had we taken Elly out of a wonderful,
loving Christian orphanage in Shillong simply to have her
adopted in New Delhi by a non-Christian family? How
were we not told of this requirement before beginning Elly's
transfer to Ashran?

But that was not the only new revelation. Michelle and I
would now be required to prove that we were infertile in
order to adopt a child from India. Again, why was this

information only now being revealed, almost three years into our adoption? Wasn't this important criterion that needed to be shared before an adoption got underway? We were reeling from all of this bad news. But, once again, the Way-Maker was preparing a way over these road bumps.

Early in Michelle's cancer treatment, her doctor had informed us that any future pregnancy would not be beneficial to her long-term health. Desiring to heed this advice, and also because we had our family established with Andrew, Abby, and Elly on the way, I chose to have a vasectomy. Little did I know that two years later, this decision would be pivotal in helping secure our adoption of Elly. My general practitioner was more than willing to write a letter on our behalf, stating that we were unable to have additional children.

Michelle and I struggled through the several months Elly was available for adoption to Indian families. As required by Indian law, ads were placed both online and in various papers stating that Elly could be adopted. We were told that it was unusual for an Indian family to want to adopt an older child, but we were nervous, nonetheless. Friends and family prayed with us for this time to pass with no inquiries.

Autumn leaves once again began to change colors in Crystal Lake. Fall has always been my favorite time of year. But, this season, I was too preoccupied with worry over Elly's situation to enjoy God's beautiful creation surrounding me. One afternoon, as I was beginning my cool-down following a run in our neighborhood, I felt God's voice speak to my heart.

"Look at that tree," was the instruction. So, I paid particular attention to one of the magnificently colored oaks ahead of me that was flush with beautiful fall leaves. At that moment, a strong wind began to blow, and a multitude of leaves was launched into the air and into a downward spiral to earth.

"Follow that leaf, that one right there. Follow it all the way to the ground and pick it up," I heard. So, I kept a sharp eye on one single leaf as it gently floated to the ground, landing in the vicinity of thousands of other leaves exactly like it. But I had watched carefully, and I knew which one I was to retrieve. I picked up the leaf; the next words pierced my heart to the core.

"This leaf represents Elly, whom I have chosen for you from among all others." I was immediately broken and began to weep. Just a short time later, we were informed that Elly would officially become ours. Time had expired, and no Indian family had stepped forward.

I still have Elly's leaf.

That fall, our weekly routine included a Saturday evening call to Elly in India. Until this point, we had limited communication with her – just a few messages or photos conveyed by intermediaries. With Elly's developing English skills, our conversations would follow a familiar script.

"How are you?"
"I am fine."
"What did you do today?"
"I took care of the babies."
"We love you!"
"I love you!"
"Goodbye."
"Goodbye."

In December 2003, I sensed the need to make a trip to New Delhi to push the adoption process across the finish line. I would meet with our attorney to finalize any lingering legal matters still requiring completion. I would then meet Mrs. Franklin, the orphanage director, to work out final transfer arrangements for Elly. And, I would finally be meeting Elly for the first time!

My trip was scheduled to take place early in the month. Our attorney agreed to meet me at the New Delhi airport to transport me to my hotel. When I arrived in New Delhi well past midnight after almost two days of travel, the arrival hall was full of happy Indians ready to take me anywhere I wanted to go—but there was no sign of my lawyer. It was now so late, and I was so tired that I decided to leave connecting with the attorney until the next day. I was able to find a taxi driver who spoke broken English. I communicated that I needed a hotel in the part of the city where our attorney had his office. I'm not sure that my instructions mattered, because I am certain I was taken to a fleabag hotel belonging to one of his relatives. While this "establishment" was not the type of place I would normally stay at three in the morning, I was exhausted and did not protest. All I wanted was a place to lay my head and sleep. Everything would look better in the morning. I stepped into my dingy room and collapsed on the bed, not to awaken until mid-day.

I telephoned Upamanyu's office and informed him that I would be calling on him early that afternoon. We never discussed the airport incident the evening before. Playing the role of "ugly American" accomplished very little, even when I was paying the bills. Upamanyu and I knew each other fairly well after months of emails and telephone conversations, and it was nice to finally meet him in person. Our relationship felt comfortable, as if we were continuing something that had started some time ago.

Upamanyu informed me that things were progressing nicely in regard to our final paperwork. One last court decision was required in order to make the adoption official in India, and I would soon be meeting with Upamanyu's colleague, who was in charge of submitting our last set of documents to the court. Upamanyu took me to a much nicer hotel where I would be staying for the remainder of my time in New Delhi, and we agreed to see each other once more before I left town.

I was eventually driven to the governmental court building where Upamanyu's colleague had his office. It is difficult to describe the scene I witnessed upon entering his workplace. There were walls and walls filled with binders, with files and papers pouring out of each one. Stacks of papers lined the floor, and general office clutter was everywhere. As I sat to discuss our final document submission to the court, this colleague pulled out my binder from the massive shelf behind him. He began rifling through the reams of documents I had spent so many hours signing and compiling, getting notarized, and then notarized again. I watched in horror as he ripped with gusto page after page out of my file folder. "We won't be needing this one," he would say. "No, that one's not necessary," he declared, as the pages were torn out and thrown to the ground. While I never verbalized these words, inside, I was shouting, "That one took me four months to complete. Can't you hold on to it just in case?!"

As we finished our afternoon together, I was confident that we were truly entering the final stage of this adoption. Preparing to leave, I was not expecting the final question I was asked. "So, would you like the rest of this process through the courts to go fast or slow?" Not understanding the reason for this question, I told him that, of course, after three painstaking years, I wanted it to go fast. "Well then, a facilitation fee will be required to get your documents to the top of the court's docket." When I arrive in heaven, I will once again repent in person for what came next, but I did not hesitate to pay that few hundred dollars.

My last day in New Delhi was absolutely perfect. It was my day at the Ashran orphanage. Mrs. Franklin welcomed me to the home, and we spent the first hour discussing the final phase of the adoption process we were now entering. We also discussed that once things were finalized, Michelle and I would be returning to India together to pick up Elly. After our work was completed, I was left alone in Mrs. Franklin's office while she went to get Elly. I was about to meet my soon-to-be daughter.

I cannot describe the joy in my heart when I was finally able to take this beautiful little girl in my arms. The remainder of our day was filled with drawing pictures together, talking as much as possible, Elly introducing me to her friends, and giving me a tour of the orphanage. With great pride, Elly showed me the baby room, where she helped take care of the little ones. I met the staff of the orphanage as well, and I was able to share with them how grateful Michelle and I were for their good care of Elly. Time flew so quickly that it seemed only an instant until I needed to leave. Saying goodbye was difficult, but I was now returning home with new vigor and zeal to get this adoption completed. After a final meeting with Upamanyu, I was back home to celebrate Christmas with my family – minus one.

Christmas 2003 was exciting. Elly's arrival was imminent. The family was now fully concentrating on preparing to welcome Elly to the Manns. With Michelle's cancer treatment successfully completed a year earlier, the two of us were excitedly looking ahead to the promise of a new daughter being fulfilled in our lives and our household.

But, like so often had happened to date in this adoption, January brought not only a new year, but a new year of waiting. We received word from our lawyer that everything was completed, but there was one small remaining glitch. Apparently, the Ashran Hope Foundation, where I had visited, and Elly was living in New Delhi, had neglected to renew their orphanage license with the state. Their license had expired at the end of December 2003. Adoption papers could not be finalized until the registration of the orphanage was once again in good standing. This development was almost too much for me to bear. We had come so far, and something so minor was now our only hurdle to overcome. As I discussed the next steps with the orphanage director, Mrs. Franklin, it was all I could do to maintain my composure. She assured me that this was a minor setback that would be quickly resolved and that our adoption of Elly would take place in no time.

But the process for renewing Ashran's license did not move quickly. My frustration grew as we waited, day after day, as winter turned to spring. But one glorious spring morning, the news that we had waited over three years to hear finally arrived. Come to India and pick up your daughter!

Michelle and I quickly made plans to leave for New Delhi in mid-April of 2004. As Michelle's parents, Neil and Sue, and our kids said goodbye to us, everyone was overjoyed that we would be returning with a new family member.

Landing in India's capital, Michelle and I made our way to the same hotel in which I had previously stayed. A meeting was set with Upamanyu to pick up our paperwork that would be required in the days ahead, and then we made plans to claim Elly from the orphanage the following day.

Arriving at the orphanage was a surreal experience. This time, we would be departing with a new family member! A party-like atmosphere filled the air, as both staff and children recognized that this was a special day. Seeing Elly interact for the last time with her friends was sweet, and the knowledge that we would no longer be separated was an indescribable emotion. We had packed party supplies from the US, and before we left the orphanage that day, we made sure to have one grand celebration with all of her friends.

The staff prepared one small bag for Elly with all of her earthly belongings. As we began to say our goodbyes, we looked up to the second-floor balcony of the orphanage to see all of the children waving and shouting farewell. Elly's response was precious as she ran closer to them, smiling from ear to ear, waving and blowing final kisses.

Our next few days in New Delhi were spent getting acquainted with our new daughter, sightseeing together, purchasing Elly new clothes for the trip home, and formalizing documentation with the US embassy. It was a fun time with just the three of us getting to know each other before additional family members would soon be added to the equation. April 17, 2004, will forever be known as Elly's "Gotcha Day," the day she officially joined our family.

As our plane went "wheels up," leaving New Delhi on our flight home to Chicago, I finally allowed myself to breathe a sigh of relief and utter a prayer of thanks to the Lord. God had divinely provided for Michelle and me as we had walked through fire the previous three years – and His promise to our family was now sitting in the airplane seat between us, watching cartoons.

CHAPTER EIGHT
FORTY MORE YEARS IN THE WILDERNESS

The year 2004 was a wonderful time for our family. Elly adjusted quickly to her new clan as well as her new life in America. Mom, Dad, Andrew, and Abby were also adjusting to having a new member in the household. While there were challenges blending our family, Elly's lovely disposition made the adjustment for everyone easy.

The work of Global Business Assist was growing. Cooperative programming with International Aid Services in Africa was now commonplace. GBA efforts had also expanded to India, and the country of Ghana would soon become a recipient of GBA's business expertise. I was enjoying the new work, and I felt challenged and satisfied with how the Lord was directing and leading our efforts to empower Christians through business training in so many diverse international locations. GBA's move into supporting and managing microfinance programs in both Ghana and South Sudan was especially exciting. It was amazing to see first-hand how building capacity in individuals could change entire communities. A lack of finances for the organization remained a problem, but the excitement of what we were accomplishing kept Michelle and me motivated.

Since returning from our time as missionaries in Albania, Michelle had continued to assist a German organization working in southern Albania, Nehemiah Gateway (NG). Michelle traveled on an annual basis to the Nehemiah offices in Pogradec, Albania, to conduct a yearly audit for the nonprofit. Michelle also made herself available to the organization as a consultant as needed.

Because of this ongoing relationship, and because of NG's interest in what Michelle and I were now doing through GBA, we were invited to conduct a business training seminar for NG leadership in Albania during the summer of 2005. Throughout that spring, I worked to put together a teaching team and a social impact component for our trip. It was decided in my conversations with the NG staff in Albania that we would conduct a dental clinic at the same time as our seminars in a rural and impoverished Albanian village called Peshkëpi. I recruited our personal dentist, Kevin Wegrzyn, a seasoned traveler for these types of dental clinics, to join us. Over the years, Kevin and I traveled the world together, utilizing his skills.

Just prior to our August departure date for Albania, I received an urgent call from my Texas family that Mom had experienced what everyone assumed was a stroke. I determined that I needed to be with my parents as soon as possible. I immediately took a flight to Dallas, praying the entire trip for Mom's recovery. She was being treated at a local hospital in Denton, Texas, the hometown of my youth.

Within a few hours of landing in Dallas, I was by Mom's bedside in the hospital. She didn't look good, but she recognized me immediately and seemed glad to see me. Over the next few days, we discovered the doctors had made an unfortunate error in their diagnosis upon admitting Mom to the hospital. Because she had displayed stroke-like symptoms in the emergency room, her attending physicians treated her as if she had suffered a stroke. But the tests, which should have been conducted much earlier, revealed Mom's condition was viral. Mom had viral encephalitis, which is an inflammation of the brain. The delay in treating her for a viral infection was not good, and we were now hoping and praying that any potential damage to Mom's brain would be minimal, or at least able to be reversed with treatment.

Mom spent several days in the hospital. She was not herself mentally, and this was hard to process. Mom had always been an avid crossword puzzle enthusiast. In fact, she would daily complete some of the most difficult crosswords imaginable. I was amazed by her ability to figure out these puzzles that, quite frankly, confounded me.

While sitting alone with Mom in her hospital room the day following my arrival, I watched her work diligently at a crossword she had been given. We sat together in silence for the better part of an hour as she worked on her puzzle. After a long period of time, I went from across the room to Mom's bedside to look at her work. In the period of an hour, Mom had filled in one word on her puzzle. That word was "bigfoot."

I was both horrified and confused. I was horrified that this puzzle, something that had previously been easy for her, now seemed an impossible mental challenge. I was confused as to why, of all the mental connections that were not taking place in Mom's brain, she correctly answered "bigfoot." Mom's intricate and complex mind, created by the Lord, was no longer working correctly. I felt overwhelmingly sad.

Within days, Mom was allowed to leave the hospital. Her progress was slow, but we did see improvement. I returned home to Crystal Lake, thankful that my brothers, Jim and Mark, lived in the Dallas area. They were able to check on Mom and monitor her condition. Over the next week, we were often in communication with regard to how she was progressing. We were encouraged and hopeful that Mom was getting better.

As the date of my trip with Michelle and the GBA team to Albania drew closer, I was conflicted as to whether or not I should travel. I remember having a long conversation with my brother, Jim, about this, and he encouraged me to proceed with my plans. All indications were that Mom was improving, which was confirmed by her doctors. Mom would have a long road of therapy ahead, but physically, her life appeared to be out of danger. I agreed with this collective assessment and continued with my travel plans for Albania.

Our trip was excellent. Not only was GBA's business training well-received, but it was also considered to be, by the NG Director, Arnold Geiger, one of the best training sessions in which he had taken part. Our dental outreach to Peshkëpi was also a huge success. As our departure date approached, we were riding high with enthusiasm from our time in Pogradec.

The evening before our intended departure, I received a telephone call from my good friend, Bob Wittenzellner, in

Germany. Mom had passed away on the morning of August 10, 2005.

My parents had been planning a lunch date with my father's twin brother, Robert, who lived nearby, on the day she died. That morning Dad went to his office while Mom lay down for a short nap. Robert intended to pick Mom up at the house following her nap and travel with her into town for their lunch appointment, which would be followed by a doctor's visit. Mom never woke up from her nap. In a strange twist of fate, my Mom had just passed away from the same viral infection that had taken our adopted daughter, Elly's, birth mother as well.

I sat in my room, hearing this news from my dear friend, and I was devastated. I was simultaneously hit by waves of both extreme loss and guilt. I had just lost my dear mother, and I was half a world away when she died. At this moment, the world collapsed around me. Fortunately, Michelle and our host, Arnold Geiger, organized our next steps as I was now useless. Our flight was scheduled to depart Albania the next morning. Thankfully, that flight was also the first available out of the country, so there were no additional arrangements necessary to get us quickly home.

Everything that took place from that point until we got on the plane the next day was a blur to me. Someone upgraded Michelle and me to business class on our flight. Although he has denied it, I have always believed that it was our host, Arnold. It is also possible that one of our GBA traveling companions upgraded us. Regardless, that kind thought was an enormous blessing at the time. My family had informed me that the funeral service would take place in Denton in just a few days. We would need to get on a plane to Texas almost immediately upon our arrival in Chicago. I was asked to perform Mom's graveside service. I cried the entire way across the Atlantic Ocean as I attempted to compose words to say for Mom's funeral. But all that came to mind were feelings of raw emotion caused by her death. I can't imagine what those sitting near me on the flight must have thought.

Mom's service was lovely. However, our entire family was still too overcome with grief to process what had just happened to us. Mom had always been the glue that held our family together, and the hole that she left was going to be impossible to fill. Each of us processed Mom's untimely departure in a unique way. These events propelled me into a very dark chapter of my life.

Because of the disbelief and disobedience of the children of Israel following their mandate to possess the land God had promised their forefathers, the Israelites wandered in the desert for forty years until an unbelieving generation passed away. I was now entering a time in my life when God's promises no longer rang true to me. The loss of my Mom triggered doubt and uncertainty in God that also cascaded into a period of disobedience to His Word. The days ahead became my proverbial forty-year wilderness experience.

I was struggling with the fact that I was not convinced that Mom was in a better place following her death. Growing up in a Southern Baptist denominational church, I don't remember hearing many sermons concerning heaven and our life to come after we die. My image of heaven was perpetually singing hymns and praises to our Lord – for all eternity. This was how I had heard it described by countless people.

Now don't get me wrong; I love singing and praising Jesus. But, after forty minutes of worship on Sunday morning, I usually am ready to move on to whatever comes next. An eternity of singing sounds like a long time to me.

I also had the mental image of those in heaven floating around on clouds – heavenly angels playing their harps. Yes, I did watch a lot of Saturday morning cartoons growing up. The point being, I had no idea what my mother was now experiencing following her untimely departure from this earth.

I recognized that I enjoyed life on this planet, and Mom was taken away from that life way too prematurely. If I knew that what came next was better, I would miss Mom, but I would be happy for her as well. The way things stood at the moment, I only felt angry and sad.

I began to seek out and read Christian books related to heaven. None of the books I discovered were worth the effort. In fact, most were terrible. Several, if what was written in them was accurate, made me not want to go to heaven. This exercise was making me despondent toward spiritual things. My spiritual life was suffering, and I'm sure this attitude spilled over into my relationship with my family. I could not shake the malaise that had come over my soul. At a dark point during this journey, I wrote the following poem that summed up my state of being.

BLIND FAITH

The days are long. The nights are dark. No light.

Wait - light, but seen only dimly as through a fog.

It illuminates nothing. Everything is a misty haze of confusion.

I'm like a blind man – staggering, arms out, groping for something real to touch, to feel, to guide me.

In the happy-ending fairytale life I imagine, I am saved by radiance from above – it envelops me, showing me clearly the way.

But how does this journey end?

On the trail I traverse, I see nothing of what lies ahead in the darkness.

I tell myself to keep moving forward, if only because I cannot turn back.

What a hopeless poem. But it summed up life for me during this period. Finally, a light did appear on the horizon through a book written by Donald Miller titled, Blue Like Jazz. The book, which I viewed as transformational, included two concepts that opened my eyes to a new way of thinking. I'll express these concepts in the terms I used at the time to relate them to my life, but they are his ideas, not mine.

The first concept dealt with the goodness of God. Why was it that I felt I had to understand everything about heaven in order to believe that it was a better place than earth? In reality, all I needed to understand was the character and nature of God in order to believe He has good things in store for us – and for my mother as well.

My college roommate, Mike Jeffries, has always been known as "Uncle Mike" to my kids. One Christmas, Uncle Mike gave our son, Andrew, a three hundred-dollar Lego set that Andrew had dreamt of owning for months. This gift far exceeded the Christmas gift-giving price range we had for the kids. But that wasn't the least bit of concern for Uncle Mike. You should have seen Andrew's reaction when he opened that present on Christmas morning! From that moment forward, Mike was always known by our children as the giver of good gifts. In fact, that is a part of Mike's character. As long as I can remember, he has always been a giver of good things.

What do you think happened in the minds of my youngsters every Christmas thereafter when they found a gift from Uncle Mike under the Christmas tree? Even though they had absolutely no idea what was inside that present, they nonetheless knew that whatever it was, it was going to be great. Why did they know this? They knew this because they knew the character of the gift giver.

The application of this truth in my life was obvious. I understood the character of my Lord and Savior and that I could trust Him to create a good place for us in His presence one day. Trusting in the goodness of His character eliminated my need to understand everything about heaven or about what happens once I die. In fact, I now have a bold confidence that whatever happens after I die, it will far exceed the wildest dreams of my imagination.

The second simple but profound revelation Donald Miller helped me grasp was that we serve a God of infinite knowledge. Imagine the knowledge that God possesses as a very large pitcher of water. Now imagine trying to pour that pitcher of knowledge into a very small cup. Of course, the cup immediately becomes full and starts to overflow.

If this is true, that we as mere mortals do not have the capacity to hold or understand the infinite knowledge of a Creator-God, then why are we so upset when there are things that happen in this life that we do not understand? In a sense, it is rather egotistical of us to think that we should be able to understand everything that transpires in this world. Even Christ knew equality with the Father was not something to be sought (Philippians 2:6).

Blue Like Jazz helped rescue me from the dark place described in my poem "Blind Faith." I began to concentrate on knowing both God and His character. I also came to understand that my emotions, my feelings of sadness in regard to the loss of my mother, were fickle. For far too long, I had lived my life based on the feelings of the day—one day, I was dejected; the next day, I was cheerful. My emotions were controlling my spiritual contentment. Understanding the character of God provided a foundation of certainty that taught me that my happiness was not dependent upon the day's circumstances.

As an example, consider the emotion of happiness. It can be deceptive. It can either be the shallowest of emotions or one that explores the deepest depths of contentment. Happiness that has its roots in love, service to others, and the character of God will sustain me. But happiness based on the desires of a man's human condition will always leave me empty. No longer would I allow the emotions that were dictated by my immediate circumstances to control me. I began to seek fulfillment and contentment based on God and His character.

With new energy and renewed calling and passion, I continued to push full speed ahead with the vision for service that the Lord had given me. Some very dark nights of the soul had passed, but unlike my poem, the light that was guiding me was now clearly visible once again.

CHAPTER NINE
WE CAN TAKE THESE GIANTS

In the years following my mother's death, GBA's ties with International Aid Services (IAS) grew stronger. In fact, without a formalized working agreement, GBA was now conducting most of our business empowerment programs in IAS target countries, with the notable exception of Ghana. IAS staff on the ground in east Africa helped to facilitate GBA programing, and this saved our organization a large amount of administrative funding. Additionally, IAS had become a known commodity to our volunteer team, and our two organizations found ourselves working very well together.

In November of 2008, I planned a trip to Khartoum, Sudan, with Leif Zetterlund, the IAS Executive Director. Personally, I was still having a difficult time, not only with the aftermath of Mom's death but also dealing with ongoing health issues related to Michelle. From a work perspective, things were going well operationally with the organization. Financial resources, however, would remain a perpetual challenge plaguing GBA. It was with the sense of carrying a heavy burden that I embarked on this trip to Muslim-controlled northern Sudan. Even still, I was looking forward to spending time with Leif.

A component of our trip was travel to South Sudan, specifically the area of Akuem, Bahr el Ghazal. My goal was to evaluate the feasibility of a new microfinance program for the region. I was looking forward to this part of our journey. Leif had informed me that he would organize the travel details of getting to South Sudan, which was a separate country from the North.

Upon the conclusion of our meetings in Khartoum, Leif communicated that we would be driving a pickup full of supplies to South Sudan and Bahr el Ghazal. This was problematic for several reasons. First, the journey was over 1,300 miles of desolate and difficult terrain. Second, I had no travel permit to travel in northern Sudan outside of Khartoum. If we were stopped while still in the North, I would be in trouble. Third, I had no visa for South Sudan, and there was no border crossing or checkpoint anywhere near the frontier we were crossing. I would be entering a new country illegally without any documentation. Leif assured me that this would not be a problem. He said that upon our arrival, we would visit the first available customs outpost to legalize my presence in South Sudan. Knowing Leif was a veteran at this, I fully trusted him in making this decision.

Together in our IAS pickup, Leif and I set out on our journey. The first several hours after leaving Khartoum were quite enjoyable. We encountered relatively nice, paved roads that helped us make good time. But soon thereafter, the situation changed. Abruptly, after several hours of driving, Leif made a turn off the main roadway onto an unmarked path that looked like it was taking us directly into the thick of bush country. I asked Leif how he knew for sure that this was the way, and I'll never forget his response. "From this point on, we follow the sun."

To say that I was now out of my comfort zone is an understatement. I'm not sure how I thought we were going to get to South Sudan, but traveling through the bush on small dirt paths, that I found out later were created by IAS years earlier, was not on my radar. After several stops for Leif to ask the locals who were living in the middle of nowhere if we were headed in the right direction, Leif was convinced that we were on course.

The remainder of our day was filled with pleasant conversation and the occasional logistical challenge of nursing our vehicle in the attempt to climb hills and cross ravines. Never did I see a road sign or other point of navigational orientation that could help us on our journey. But amazingly, as dark began to fall, our truck pulled up to the guest cottage where Leif had intended for us to spend the night. His directional instincts couldn't have been any better had he been guided by GPS navigation.

In the next two days, we would travel over wild landscapes, and through the beautiful Nuba Mountains. IAS had done much work in this area that was still enduring occasional bombing attacks from Khartoum. Along our journey, Leif pointed out wells that IAS had drilled for the local communities. We encountered one of the most interesting sights as we entered the oil fields that border North and South Sudan. There was a Chinese city situated in one of the principal oil regions—in the heart of Africa. It was as if I had been transported to rural China. As China had taken over the management of Sudanese oil contracts, they brought in their own countrymen to do the work.

On our final day on the road, I began to feel especially depressed. So many hours to think can sometimes be a curse, and I was giving in to negative thought patterns as I remembered all of the burdens waiting for me at home.

As we entered South Sudan, I could see hundreds, if not thousands, of what I can only describe as grass-constructed tipis. I asked Leif about what I was witnessing, and he said that this area had recently experienced a major flooding disaster. All of these individuals and families had been displaced from their homes by the flood. It was staggering. There was no city in sight. There were no facilities from which they could buy or purchase food. No running water or sanitation services. No aid organizations to help. Literally, nothing was available to assist these people. Just hundreds and hundreds of poorly constructed grass shelters as far as the eye could see.

We drove through this expanse as I heard the Lord speak to me. "I want you to list your problems." Well, that was easy. I began to make a mental list of everything weighing heavily on my heart, and I felt my list was extensive. I completed this mental exercise, which I had already been working on for several hours due to my sour disposition, and once again felt the Holy Spirit's prompting. He said, "Look out your window to the right." So, I looked out the window. What I noticed were even more refugee shelters along the roadside. The Lord went in for the spiritual adjustment kill shot as I heard Him say, "Now, I want you to list their problems." I was so devastated that I never began the exercise.

My trip with Leif had solidified a friendship between the two of us. It had also strengthened the bond between GBA and IAS. In one of our numerous conversations, Leif informed me that several years previously, IAS had opened a small office in the United States. Apparently, the legal 501(c)3 nonprofit structure still existed, but it had never grown as an organization. This conversation continued throughout 2009, and Leif and I began to discuss merging our two organizations.

When the twelve spies returned from Canaan, their report was bad. The spies said, "The land we explored devours those living in it. All the people we saw there are of great size. We saw the Nephilim. We seemed like grasshoppers in our own eyes, and we looked the same to them" (Numbers 13:32–33, NIV). But only Joshua and Caleb presented a minority report. "Then Caleb silenced the people before Moses and said, 'We should go up and take possession of the land, for we can certainly do it'" (Numbers 13:30).

I was initially scared at the prospect of molding what Michelle and I had started with GBA into the broader banner of International Aid Services. But God was building a wonderful relationship, and I was sensing that IAS was the partner GBA needed to expand our reach into majority world countries. The process of merging the two organizations appeared as a giant to me that could not be overcome, but with prayer and consultation from my board of directors, it was decided that this new partnership needed to be pursued. We could take this land; we could certainly do it!

To complete the merger between our two nonprofits, we developed an action plan. The legal incorporation of GBA would continue to exist, but the organization would no longer be used. The fledgling nonprofit structure IAS had created years earlier would now be the legal structure used for all donations and all work moving forward. I would become the new IAS America president, and all of the former GBA board members would be added to the new IAS board of directors. Over the next year, corporate branding would shift from GBA to IAS, and a campaign would be run throughout the year to inform donors of the shift from GBA to the IAS family. The first official IAS America board meeting took place on April 26, 2010, in Estes Park, Colorado, at which time I was elected president of the corporation.

The next few years were spent solidifying the new IAS brand and vision with former GBA donors. Additionally, our business programing, in regard to in-country accountability and reporting, was now integrated into IAS. Overnight we increased operational capacity, which helped accomplish much of what we desired to undertake programmatically. New microfinance projects and new training programs were started. I was able to introduce our donors to the amazing well-drilling, and sanitation improvement projects throughout East Africa that IAS was completing. It was an exciting time of operational growth and personal fulfillment.

Dark clouds were, however, on the horizon. On the afternoon of July 11, 2012, an IAS team was returning from a water and education assessment project in the region of Galkayo in Puntland, Somalia. Having completed a long day of work, the IAS team (three Kenyan nationals and a local Somali IAS worker) were traveling in two vehicles, the first being an armed security escort. At approximately 5:30 pm, they came under attack by a band of fourteen Somali pirates. The pirates fired indiscriminately into the

IAS convoy, outnumbering and overpowering the three Puntland officers. Two officers suffered minor injuries from the gunfight, and our local Somali IAS worker, Axmed Isse, was critically wounded. The remaining three IAS employees (Janet Kanga, Martin Kioko, and Abdinoor Boru) were kidnapped and taken deep into a region of Somalia controlled by the pirates.

Axmed was first taken to a regional hospital but was later transported to Kenya for additional medical treatment. Upon arrival in Kenya, it was determined that the gunshot to his kidney had ruptured his colon, and he had also contracted malaria and an infection in his wounds. Within a short period of time, we received communication from the pirates that our Kenyan staff members were safe and being well-treated; however, no immediate demands were made by their captors. As we would later discover, while they might have been safe in the hands of the pirates, they were not well-treated.

Upon news of this kidnapping, the IAS Executive Committee, of which I was a member, immediately formed a crisis management team that worked daily toward the goal of the successful release of our hostages. While I was not a member of the crisis management team initially, I was kept informed of developments as a member of the IAS Executive Committee.

After this kidnapping of the IAS team in Somalia, several aid agencies, in addition to IAS, suspended their activities in Somalia due to increased security risks and the possibility of further kidnappings of our expatriate staff. With aid agencies interrupting their activities, it was the impoverished recipients of these relief efforts in Somalia who would suffer. But we could not risk putting our staff members in further danger.

Within just a few days of this horrific development, I was contacted by our Swedish office and asked to place a call to a company in the US, Nighthawk One. According to the information I was forwarded, Nighthawk One had reached out to the IAS executive leadership as a company specializing in hostage negotiation, recovery, and rescue. The company was made aware of the kidnappings through regional news reports and had reached out to the IAS corporate offices in Stockholm to offer its services. Our office in Sweden, after some initial emails back and forth with Nighthawk One's corporate leadership, asked me to call the company to discuss the possibility of Nighthawk One assisting us in the safe recovery of our staff members.

This began a series of calls I would make with the Nighthawk One president. Not long after this, Leif was included in these calls, as was a Nighthawk Once specialist named William Riley. IAS was forwarded Riley's credentials as an ex-Navy SEAL who now worked for them as an operations specialist. IAS soon engaged the services of Nighthawk One, with William managing our case.

As I was not a member of the crisis management team, my role was to facilitate their needs. I worked primarily as a go-between for IAS and Nighthawk One. After several weeks of deliberation, it was decided that Nighthawk One would travel to Somalia for an assessment of the current situation. They would take a team of operators that would be prepared to extract our hostages should the opportunity arise.

Over the next few months, Axmed, who had been shot and was in serious condition, began to recover from his wounds and infections. In relatively short order, he was released from the hospital and able to return home. Little did we realize that Axmed, with his serious injuries, would be the fortunate member of our team that was attacked.

As William Riley prepared his team for its trip to Somalia, I wired William the contracted sum for this operation. However, I made a mistake when I initiated the transfer with the bank and accidentally wired two-thirds of the agreed-upon amount. William called to inform me that he had only received partial payment from IAS, and I quickly worked to correct my mistake and wire the remaining balance owed. I hoped that this error would not reflect poorly on the relationship with Nighthawk One that was developing.

Upon Riley's arrival in Kenya, he was to meet with IAS staff on the ground and then continue travel with an IAS representative to Somalia. There they would attempt to make further contact with the pirates and evaluate potential next steps. After several days of meetings in Kenya with the IAS crisis management team, William and one of our representatives departed for Somalia. The remaining team members of Nighthawk One would fly directly to Somalia to meet William.

I was preparing for a trip to Sweden to meet with our IAS Executive Committee. The ongoing hostage crisis was at the top of our agenda. Prior to my departure, I received a telephone call from one of my IAS America board members, Stephen Kaufman. Stephen shared with me a dream he had the previous evening about William Riley. In Stephen's dream, William Riley was an imposter. While Stephen made no recommendations, he wanted to make me aware of his dream. I reassured Stephen that I had seen William's

credentials and that we had already received word from
Riley that he was on the ground in Somalia. Our first report
was that things were going well. I attempted to placate
Stephen's concerns by assuring him that he had nothing
to worry about. But, nonetheless, I stored this telephone
conversation in the back of my mind.

The next several weeks that Riley was in Somalia were
troubling. Leif and I were together in Sweden, and we
discussed each report that arrived from William. Conflicting
stories of events taking place on the ground, coupled with
inconsistencies in the information we were receiving from
other sources, made us question whether or not Riley
was effective. After weeks of promises with few positive
results, IAS requested William return to Kenya for a debrief
with our staff. During his time in Kenya, Riley met with
representatives of the hostage's families. He promised them
that he would safely recover their family members.

Our IAS team felt terrible for these families. On what was
becoming a daily basis, we would attempt to encourage
and comfort them, assuring them that we were doing
our best. These conversations were difficult. We would
go weeks without hearing from the kidnappers, all
the while not knowing the condition of the hostages.
Governmental agencies in Somalia were slow to provide
help, and the Kenyan government was simply too weak
or too overwhelmed to be of assistance. The international
community was equally noncommittal in regard to any form
of practical assistance. IAS was working for the release of
our hostages in a vacuum of engagement from other sources.

After many weeks, the kidnappers began to contact IAS on a
regular basis. Their demands were in the millions of dollars

for the release of our team members. On several occasions, we were able to negotiate the delivery of food parcels, toiletries, medicines, and other practical bits of help for our staff members. There were always problems in getting this aid delivered. We would eventually discover that the conditions under which our team members were being held were horrific. The IAS team was kept barefoot so that they could not escape into the bush of Somalia. They were never given a change of clothing. They were not allowed to change their underwear during the course of their capture. Janet was not allowed feminine hygiene products. One can only imagine the humiliation this caused in the all-male environment in which she was being held. Over the course of their captivity, they were often sick, they would lose weight to the point of being unrecognizable, and they would constantly endure the mental torture of hearing their captors discuss their imminent execution. Our team members were experiencing a living hell on earth.

While William was in Somalia, the two of us had a conversation that troubled me. William told me that, due to the danger on the streets in Somalia, he was forced to spend an inordinate amount of time inside his hotel room. I had made the statement that as a former SEAL, it must have been difficult for him to spend so much time with limited physical activity. His response was that it was no big deal. He proceeded to tell me that he spent the majority of his time playing video games. This was an immediate red flag. I instantly recalled Stephen Kaufman's dream. What type of Navy SEAL, even a former SEAL, isn't concerned about physical operational preparedness on assignment in a hostile nation?

Upon Riley's return to the US that fall of 2012, he was invited to a meeting with the IAS America board of directors. During this meeting, Nighthawk One submitted to IAS a proposal for the rescue of our hostages. I realized if we were going to continue to use the assistance of Nighthawk One, IAS must do a better job than we had previously done of vetting the company. It was necessary to know if they were truly capable of carrying out the type of operation Nighthawk One was claiming they could successfully conduct on our behalf. Upon the submission of their rescue proposal, which was a significant six-figure sum, I required a plethora of supporting documentation. I requested multiple references, biographies from staff members, and military resumes and accommodations. I also requested further conversations with the president of Nighthawk One regarding its proposal and its capacity as a company to undertake such a mission.

Upon receiving this documentation from them, I asked a board member of IAS America, Steven Boyles, a Naval Academy graduate, to vet the military information we received. Simultaneously, I began to pour through references. In the case files of missions Nighthawk One had completed, there were some incredible stories of rescue. On paper, this appeared to be the perfect company to assist us in our hostage crisis. As I called these references, I was stunned by their achievements and impressed by the high level of esteem in which each former client held both William Riley and Nighthawk One. After thoroughly investigating three rescue operations, including online searches for information, I was beginning to believe that Nighthawk One was the real deal. But, the fourth and final case I was given as a reference made me pause.

The final Nighthawk One mission given to me involved a corporate kidnapping. But, as I read through the case material, there was no contact information given for those allegedly involved. Nor was I able to substantiate any of the purported incidents via news articles available online. For a case this significant, there would certainly have had to have been at least one story in the press. Additionally, the person listed as the CEO of the corporation who had been purportedly kidnapped was a ghost. I could find no record of such a person having held the position of CEO for this corporation.

While I was investigating these references, Steven Boyles had requested help from a few of his military friends. Going through the military resumé William Riley provided, Steven's associates had discovered some significant inconsistencies. For example, William had said that he was stationed at a military installation during a period of time when this particular base had been closed. Additionally, Riley claimed that he had earned medals while in the Navy that actually belonged to a different military branch – the Coast Guard. Things were not adding up. Steven requested I ask William for his DD214, which is an official record, or transcript, of a veteran's time in the armed forces. With these inconsistencies coming to light, Steven had a colleague put him in contact with Don Shipley. Don was a former Navy SEAL, and also an expert in exposing those impersonating his brothers-in-arms.

With so many irregularities now surfacing, it was at this point that the dam broke for William Riley and Nighthawk One. Steven and I requested William join us on a conference call to discuss our concerns about the documentation that they had provided IAS. Unbeknownst to William, we invited

Don Shipley to join us in this conversation. This telephone call was recorded, and it remains a favorite on Don Shipley's website, exposing phony Navy SEALS.

While Riley did not confess to impersonating a SEAL or running a fraudulent organization on this telephone conversation, within a half-hour, William rang Don Shipley and admitted his deception. When William Riley's DD214 was eventually received by IAS, it exposed the fact that Riley had never been a SEAL during his time in the US Navy. It was also discovered that William had spent the majority of his military service under arrest in the Naval Consolidated Brig, Miramar. We had been completely duped.

While IAS had lost a significant amount of money with William Riley and Nighthawk One, that was not the real travesty. IAS had wasted several months of valuable time on this bogus individual and his mock company. During this time, our team members were languishing in captivity in Somalia.

This man, on behalf of his company, had visited the families of these hostages promising to recover their children. He had given them false hope, all in order to financially profit from their desperate situation. While we would continue to focus our full attention on securing the release of our coworkers, I would not let William Riley go unpunished for what he had done. I have always regretted falling for this con, no matter how expertly perpetrated it was on IAS.

Over the course of the next several years, I worked with both the FBI and the Justice Department to hold William Riley accountable for his actions. Unfortunately, his co-conspirators in Nighthawk One escaped justice. As most of our organizational interaction had taken place with William

Riley, there was not enough evidence against his partner, the professed president of the company. Additionally, we later discovered that William's "team" in Somalia was comprised of one individual. This man was an ex-prison guard Riley had met while in jail.

Eventually, Riley did pay for his deception. William Riley served over three years in federal prison and was required to make restitution to the organization. Because of the mistake I made in wiring funds twice to William before his trip to Somalia, Riley was charged by the Justice Department with not one, but two counts of wire fraud.

Following Riley's return from Somalia, I contacted a good family friend from our time in Albania. Dave Fyock worked with Mission Aviation Fellowship (MAF). Dave was able to put me in touch with a hostage negotiator who had formerly been employed by a major metropolis on the West Coast. This gentleman, Bob, now spent his time helping organizations like ours with missionaries in trouble. Bob had helped MAF on several occasions, and he came highly recommended. Having full confidence in Dave and his assessment of Bob and his abilities, I immediately contacted Bob to see if he might be available to assist IAS.

Bob was introduced to our crisis management team and almost immediately engaged in helping us secure the safe return of our staff members. Bob did not have an enviable job. A ten-hour time difference between the West Coast and Somalia meant that Bob was often making calls to the pirates in the middle of the night. It took much communication on Bob's part to develop a rapport with the hostage-takers. Many times, Bob had trouble not only understanding the dynamics of whom he was speaking with but even understanding who was in charge. Piracy is a fluid business. Often, hostages are sold from one group of pirates to the next. Months went by with occasional signs of hope, but then periods of no progress at all. Everyone on the crisis management team was frustrated, and it was even harder for the families of the hostages. And still, no government would come to our assistance.

The hostage crises dragged on, and I was appointed the new Chairman of the IAS Executive Committee. I also began to participate more often in crisis management team meetings. For all of us, especially Leif, who carried the brunt of this burden as Executive Director of IAS, these days were dark. Often, when I was out enjoying a good time with my family, I remembered our team members who were huddled under a tree with no shoes, no food, and in the same clothes they had been wearing on the day of their capture. I would feel instantly guilty for enjoying my life while my colleagues were in such a desperate state. Everything that took place in my life throughout 2013 had the shadow of this hostage crisis hanging over it.

During my time as Chairman of the IAS Executive Committee, I began to help IAS work toward a leadership transition in the organization. Leif's son, Daniel, an attorney, had been a key player in the organization for years. Leif desired a diminished role in the top leadership of the organization, and Daniel was the logical alternative. How this transition would work, and when it would take place were all issues the Executive Committee would need to decide. No transition would take place, however, until our hostage crisis had concluded.

Bob and the crisis management team continued to look for ways to free our hostages. At the same time, the work of IAS had to continue. In April of 2013, I was asked to make a trip to Ethiopia to help evaluate a business empowerment project and to inspect some IAS wells that were being drilled in a remote region of the country. This would be my first trip to Ethiopia, and I was excited to visit our office and meet the entire IAS Ethiopian team. Packing for my journey, I remember thinking about my many years of good fortune while traveling. In my twenty-five years of travel, although I had encountered some harrowing experiences, I had never been involved in a serious accident while on the road. Considering the conditions of the roads throughout most of the majority world, this was unusual. I didn't dwell on this thought—I simply remember it going through my mind.

Once in Ethiopia, we visited the Oromia/Borena region of the country, some 700 kilometers south of the capital Addis Ababa on the Ethiopian/Kenyan border. It was encouraging to see a new well being drilled that would bring fresh, clean water to this region. Residents were currently walking many miles to obtain water, unsuitable for drinking. Villagers would now be able to allow their daughters to go to school. No longer would they be required to spend their days fetching water from a distant source. Understanding the ripple effect this one well would have on health, education, personal livelihood, and so many other facets of life brought joy to my spirit.

Our journey south had been long. The roads had not been good, but our driver, who was also the director of our IAS office in Ethiopia, was excellent. Bony, in fact, was one of the best drivers I have known in all my travels—and this was a serious compliment. We finished our business on the Kenyan border and began our return to Addis. It was decided that we would stay overnight in the city of Awasa before continuing onward to the capital.

It had been a long day of driving, but Bony had navigated the roadways with expertise. In fact, at one point, children playing together on the shoulder of the road dashed out onto the roadway without looking. Bony easily avoided what could have been a catastrophe. I felt safe in his hands.

At twilight, we approached the city of Awasa. We had made it. The discomfort of a long travel day would soon be eased by a nice dinner and then a restful night's sleep in a decent hotel, something we had not enjoyed in Oromia/Borena. Bony took us to a superb restaurant, and we all left with happy and full stomachs. Now, all that was between us and a good night's sleep was a five-minute drive to our evening's accommodations.

As we drove through the downtown streets of Awasa, I was sitting in the back of our SUV, laughing and joking with my traveling companions from Sweden--Fredrik and Anton. We were enjoying ourselves after such a nice dinner and the prospects of this long day soon being over. I glanced their way, discussing some non-important issues as I felt a strong jolt to the vehicle. We came to an immediate, screeching halt. My first thought was that we had hit an animal crossing the road—but it was much worse.

We would only learn the full story of what had just transpired hours later. A drunk, elderly man had been staggering along the poorly lit roadway for the past half hour. Several times he had ventured into the street but had been pulled back to the sidewalk by a concerned passerby.

Tragically, it happened one final time when there was no one to save him from danger.

Bony was driving under the speed limit with his eyes on the road and not distracted in the slightest at the time of the accident. All of the streetlights in this portion of the city were non-functional, and this man's abrupt departure from the sidewalk into the middle of the roadway left Bony with little time to react. We all jumped out of the vehicle. In a country where emergency services are not dependable, the man was placed into the back of the SUV, and Bony sped away to the hospital. Fredrick, Anton, and I were left by the side of the road, shaken by the event. We took a cab to our hotel, where we waited to hear the outcome of this tragic incident.

Sadly, the elderly man died in the hospital a few days later. Although there had been several witnesses to the event who cleared Bony of any wrongdoing, Bony was put in jail for several days. In a country where almost everything runs on bribery, an incident like this was extremely unfortunate. Over the next few months, it was only because of Bony's connections that he experienced no further repercussions. Even though he was not at fault in the events of that evening, Bony was required to pay the family a sum in the thousands of dollars for the loss of their family member. I often think of this horrific day, and I am grateful that I was busy talking with my colleagues in the back seat at the time of the calamity and did not witness the incident.

Our hostage situation moved into 2014, and Bob and the crisis management team appeared to be making progress. After so many months in captivity, there was finally a glimmer of hope on the horizon for the successful release of our team members.

On June 5, 2014, Leif Zetterlund, the Executive Director of International Aid Services, issued the following press release:

"On the 11th of July 2012, at approximately 5:30 pm, an IAS team was attacked by an armed group of people near Galcayo in Puntland, Somalia. The team was traveling in two vehicles, including an escort car with three armed Puntland police officers who bravely defended the IAS staff but were overpowered by a much larger group of attackers. All of the police officers recovered from injuries sustained during the attack, as did one IAS employee who was injured but not kidnapped.

This abduction of Janet Muthoni Kanga, Martin Mutisya Kioko, and Abdinoor Dabaso Boru has been condemned by both the Kenyan and Puntland governments, as well as by a number of religious leaders of many faiths. IAS immediately formed a crisis management team that has worked since the day of the kidnapping to find a resolution to this event. A number of organizations and people, both public and private, also provided invaluable assistance to IAS during this twenty-two-month crisis. For security reasons, IAS cannot name these organizations and people – but they know who they are, and we are extremely grateful for their assistance.

IAS would like to extend its deepest thanks to the families of these three hostages. Despite their overwhelming desire to do almost anything to get their family members back, they extended their trust to the IAS crisis management team. These family members supported the crisis team's decisions, and they even provided IAS with invaluable information, which proved to be very helpful in finalizing the arrangements for the release of the hostages.

The hostages were released by their kidnappers near the city of Galcayo, today on the 5th of June 2014. With the assistance of the United Nations and the Galmudug government, the hostages were taken to a safe location until they will be flown back to Nairobi and reunited with their families and friends, and debriefed. Although all will undergo routine medical screenings, we believe that they are uninjured and under the circumstances, in reasonably good health. During the period of their captivity, the IAS crisis management team was able to speak to the hostages on a number of occasions and was able to arrange the delivery of supplies from time to time.

The IAS crisis management team conducted discussions with many persons claiming to be holding these hostages during this twenty-two-month ordeal. In most cases, callers were quickly identified as frauds and dismissed. Extended discussions with the actual kidnappers resulted in the release of the hostages reported today. The kidnappers claimed to be Somali pirates, and IAS developed no information to discredit that claim.

IAS staff, alongside colleagues with other international NGOs, continue to work in Somalia, Puntland, and other dangerous locations around the world. We remain concerned about the increase of attacks on humanitarian workers, not only in Somalia but also in the broader region where IAS operates. We are committed to take necessary steps to mitigate risks for our own staff and to also engage in the wider discussion on ensuring staff safety in vulnerable and hostile environments."

Nairobi, June 5, 2014
Leif Zetterlund
Executive Director, International Aid Services

One unreported fact related to the release of our hostages had to do with the simultaneous and ongoing negotiations the United Nations was having for a separate set of hostages. This was a group of victims taken by Somali pirates from a ship years earlier. All of the citizens still held in captivity were from majority world nations that could not afford to pay ransom. After years in captivity, the UN had finally taken up their cause.

IAS was fortunate that both our staff and the UN hostages were going to be released at the same time. Because of this, the UN agreed to also help facilitate the transfer of our hostages. The moment of transition from captivity to freedom is always a very delicate and costly stage of any hostage drama, and IAS was thrilled to have the expertise of the UN assisting us in this final handover.

It is difficult to describe the joy I felt meeting Janet, Martin, and Abdinoor several months later in Nairobi. While I was just a small part of a much larger team, the successful conclusion to this twenty-two-month nightmare is one of the happiest moments in my career. I rejoice that they are now living their lives in fullness with family and friends.

CHAPTER TEN
JERICHO MARCH

In the heyday of alternative Christian music, a singer named
Steve Taylor wrote a song entitled "Jesus is for Losers." The
song goes in part:

If I was driven
Driven ahead by some noble ideal
Who took the wheel?

If I was given
Given a glimpse of some glorious road
When was it sold?

So caught up in the chase
I keep forgetting my place

Just as I am
I am stiff-necked and proud
Jesus is for losers
Why do I still play to the crowd?

Just as I am
Pass the compass, please
Jesus is for losers
I'm off about a hundred degrees

If I was groping
Groping around for some ladder to fame
I am ashamed

If I was hoping
Hoping respect would make a sturdy footstool
I am a fool

Bone-weary every climb
Blindsided every time

Just as I am
I am needy and dry
Jesus is for losers
The self-made need not apply

Just as I am
In a desert crawl
Lord, I'm so thirsty
Take me to the waterfall.

That's it. Christianity in a nutshell. The constant battle between self and selflessness. The crutch of the "sturdy footstool" of success that Steve Taylor so adequately describes drove me for a long time. It wasn't wealth or power that I sought. Instead, I sought respect – respect for being a "man of God" who accomplished great things in His name.

Thrust into leadership at an early age; I felt that it was essential that I proved myself to show that I was right for the job. What I didn't understand was that God was not looking for the self-made; rather, He was seeking a son who would be obedient. I regret that it took me so long to understand this truth.

On this Jericho March of life, one of the more pleasant surprises has been that, although it took me some time to comprehend God's priorities, my kids have understood those priorities from an early age. All children learn from their parents, but I am privileged to be able to say that I have also learned much from my offspring.

"Now the gates of Jericho were securely barred because of the Israelites. No one went out and no one came in. Then the Lord said to Joshua, 'See, I have delivered Jericho into your hands, along with its king and its fighting men'" (Joshua 6:1–2, NIV). Following the will and the direction of the Father leads to His plans being fulfilled in your life. Or, in other words, victory.

Our children are grown now, commanding seagoing vessels and harnessing nuclear power. They are well underway with life as adults. Andrew, Abby, and Elly have shown me that the Spirit of the Lord rises in each of them. As they have grown into leaders, they all have discovered principles for living that make this dad proud. An empowering drive, a sensitive spirit, and a value of hard work and generosity mark the lives they're building.

Since his early teenage years, Andrew wanted to join the Navy. Without a mariner bloodline in the family, this life path was new territory for us. Andrew was required to work hard at overcoming many obstacles that stood in the way of his Naval career, but he did so with excellence. After graduating from Iowa State, Andrew joined the ranks of the United States Navy with his first duty post on the destroyer USS Farragut. (Many thoughts go through the mind when one's son takes his station on a ship named for Admiral David Farragut, whose most famous wartime strategy was, "Damn the torpedoes. Full speed ahead!").

As he advanced in his career as a surface warfare officer, Andrew's second assignment in the Navy was on the aircraft carrier, USS Abraham Lincoln. Following a deployment to the Arabian Sea and the Persian Gulf, Andrew invited his grandfather, Neil Woodley, and me to join him on what the Navy calls a "Tiger Cruise." A Tiger Cruise is when family members get to join their sailor on the last leg of his or her deployment – in this case, a journey from Honolulu, Hawaii, to the ship's homeport of San Diego, California. One of my lifelong regrets is that I was unable to accompany Andrew due primarily to the length of the journey and my work obligations. However, his retired grandfather, Neil, was ecstatic to join this opportunity of a lifetime.

Together for almost two weeks, Neil shadowed Andrew as he went about his duties. They enjoyed each other's company, even though they were required to spend numerous hours of downtime together in close quarters.

Upon his return, Neil told me this story:

One of the young sailors under Andrew's command had screwed up royally. An action he had neglected to take had caused damage to one of the ship's systems, requiring both expense and maintenance. Andrew's Master Chief brought the young sailor into Andrew's office for his chewing out, and Neil was able to witness the entire scene.

The young sailor, most likely still a teenager, entered his commanding officer's office with fear in his eyes and prepared for the worst. But rather than berate the seaman, Andrew gently and calmly walked him through the incident, instructing him why his job was so important to the ship. By the end of the meeting, the sailor not only knew what he had done wrong, but he also had a better understanding of his value within the mission.

Neil said that he had never been more impressed with the leadership displayed by his grandson. Although Andrew was ultimately responsible for the failings of the men and women under him, he chose to empower and build up those under his command rather than tear them down.

Strong leaders also need a sensitive spirit of compassion. During the time that my children were teenagers, our church in the Chicago suburbs doubled as a homeless shelter once a week. As it was far too cold during the winter months for the homeless to be outdoors, community churches housed the homeless on a rotating schedule. By rotating evenings, local churches were able to provide shelter for the displaced for an entire week.

My girls and I volunteered to work setup for this shelter each Friday evening throughout the winter. Our job was to rearrange the church furniture for the arriving guests, prepare the dining tables for an evening meal that would be served, and distribute bed linens and mattresses for approximately thirty-five men and ten women. It was not unusual that an entire homeless family would show up at the church.

One evening, as part of our setup routine, the girls and I were asked to distribute the pillows and blankets to each mattress that was lined up in rows. To avoid having visitors take multiple blankets (there were not enough blankets for everyone to have two), we were asked to throw the pillows and blankets onto each awaiting mattress in advance of the arrival of our guests.

After we returned home, we began to discuss our volunteer experience. We talked about what it would be like to be homeless, and we imagined what sleeping at the church on a lumpy mattress together with forty others on a cold winter night might be like. Abby shared with us a thought that might have come straight from the throne room of the King of Kings.

Abby contemplatively mentioned to Elly and me that we should no longer simply throw the pillows and blankets onto the mattresses. Rather, we should neatly arrange them for each guest.

I am embarrassed to say that this had never crossed my mind. Thinking through her comments, I imagined myself being forced to enter that shelter out of extreme need, with most of my dignity having been stripped away at the front door. What if I had to bring my own family into that place? How helpless and hopeless would I feel? Under those circumstances, one of the first things I would encounter would be my "bed," waiting for me with the haphazardly thrown blanket and pillow on it.

All these years later, I still think about Abby's comments. Her thoughts remind me of her sensitive spirit toward the needs of others and the poor. With over 400 verses in the Bible concerning the poor, Abby has latched on to what moves God's heart. I've watched her share love with the needy in Africa, and I see the way she cares for both the stranger and the neighbor next door.

After graduating from the US Coast Guard Academy, Abby is now a distinguished officer in the United States Coast Guard. On a daily basis, Abby is required to guide and lead sailors who are under her authority. As she leads others, she does so with an orientation of compassion, seeing the needs of the people who are behind their uniforms and, even in leadership, exercising a sensitive spirit.

A person is not necessarily born a strong leader. It is hard work. No one works harder or has a more generous nature than our daughter, Elly. When Elly arrived in the Mann household in the spring of 2004, things began to change and change quickly. While Andrew and Abby had always been required to do household chores, those chores were simple and in proportion to what Michelle and I thought was within their limited capacity. But Elly brought with her an entirely new meaning to the word "capacity."

Elly, having lived most of her childhood in an orphanage, was no stranger to work. When I say work, I mean real work. The other two would groan and complain as they struggled to complete their Saturday responsibilities. Elly could not be given enough tasks to complete. Very quickly, Michelle and I recognized that not only was Elly an incredibly hard worker, but our expectations of our other two children needed to be seriously re-evaluated. Elly was a dynamo of enthusiasm, and she was always the first to volunteer or help when anything was needed.

Fast-forwarding to Elly's scholastic endeavors, this young lady was unstoppable. Although Elly's English skills were good when she arrived in America, they still needed improvement. This in no way stopped her from excelling in almost every area of academia. In fact, everything seemed a challenge that she relished accepting.

As a young teen, Elly marched into the house proudly informing both Michelle and me that she would from now on be babysitting the neighbor's young children. Although we had never discussed such an idea, Elly had decided on her own that she needed a job, and she had visited the neighbors to secure her employment. She was not too happy when we made her march right back and tenure her resignation from a job that she had secured only minutes earlier.

Elly has always worked hard. But in addition to her hard work, she has a generous nature that most often puts the needs of others first. In our family, Elly will be the first to offer her assistance, her time, or her money. While few people work as hard as she does to earn an income, Elly will also be the first to give it away should she perceive a need. She holds with open hands everything she owns.

Elly's hard work has helped her reach her career goals and aspirations. Elly graduated from the University of Alabama and is a chemical and biological engineer working in the nuclear power industry. Her job is so complex that I have a hard time understanding what it is that she actually does. Elly recognizes one of the greatest lessons I could ever teach my children, and that is that you can never out-give God.

Leadership. Unless you become a conduit of the heart of God, you're doomed to failure. You can be a hard worker who empowers others, but without the compassionate and giving spirit of the Father, you are self-made. And, as Steve Taylor says, "The self-made need not apply."

Just as you are
Just a wretch like me
Jesus is for losers
Grace from the blood of a tree

Just as we are
At a total loss
Jesus is for losers
Broken at the foot of the cross.[1]

---

1 Steve Taylor, "Jesus is for Losers," *Squint 1993*, Warner Alliance.

EPILOGUE

Throughout this adventure, I hope that I've learned a thing or two about leadership. Actually, there was really only one leadership lesson I needed to learn. I realized that the process of learning how to lead turned out to be learning how to serve. It is only in being a true servant that we have the capacity to be real leaders. One of the best ways we can serve others is by channeling for them the heart of God. It is a lofty aspiration, but when those we lead look our direction, may they see the Spirit of the Lord Jesus active in our lives.

Joshua 6:15–16 (NIV) states, "On the seventh day, they got up at daybreak and marched around the city seven times in the same manner, except that on that day they circled the city seven times. The seventh time around, when the priests sounded the trumpet blast, Joshua commanded the army, 'Shout! For the Lord has given you the city!'"

My prayer is that my life's path will one day be looked at as a Jericho March of obedience. Any ground that has been taken from the enemy was solely because God gave us that territory, and we were obedient to march into it. For me, this book serves as a witness to God's faithfulness in my life. It is evidence of how, over and over again, God's provision for my family and me has been sufficient. He has proven Himself time and time again as we have stepped out in faith and obedience to the call of His voice. The course through which Michelle and I have navigated has not been perfect, and it has not been easy. It has had its ups and downs, its high tides and low tides. But through it all, I can make the proclamation that God's grace has carried me – and He has carried my family as well.

These days, as I walk along trails in the Colorado high country, I often see cairns, or man-made piles of stone stacked one on top of another to mark the way or indicate the correct route. This story is my cairn. This was my path; this was the trail that I traveled. And, it is my testament to the glory of God in my life throughout the journey.

To learn more about the author, visit
www.DouglasMann.com